DOG BREEDING

The reasons that prompt people to embark on the fascinating adventure of breeding dogs are many and varied. However modest or ambitious a breeder you may aim to be, the same problems have to be faced, the same principles applied, if healthy puppies are to be raised successfully. Mr. Fitch Daglish was known internationally as a leading authority on all aspects of dog breeding. The guidance he has given in this handbook cannot fail to be of great practical value to all engaged in the fascinating task of breeding and rearing puppies, either for pleasure or profit. He has provided answers to the many problems which may arise to cause anxiety or perplexity to the novice dealing with a first litter, and offers much expert advice for the benefit of the more experienced.

Frontispiece Pharoah Hound with babies

DOG BREEDING

by
E. FITCH DAGLISH

Revised by
ANNE MACDONALD

FOYLES HANDBOOKS
LONDON

First published 1961
Reprinted 1964
Reprinted 1966
Reprinted 1968
Reprinted 1970
Reprinted 1973
Revised edition 1975
Reprinted 1978
Reprinted 1980

ISBN 0 7071 0505 6

Printed and bound in Great Britain
at The Pitman Press, Bath

CONTENTS

Photographs:
The Frontispiece and plates 1, 3, 5, 6, 7, 8, 10 and 11 by Anne Cumbers.

LIST OF ILLUSTRATIONS

CHAPTER 1

BREEDING TO AN IDEAL

THE REASONS that prompt people to embark on the fascinating adventure of breeding dogs are many and varied. It may be that a bitch puppy originally acquired purely as a pet becomes so handsome and dearly loved as she matures that the desire to produce others like her becomes irresistible. Or the spectacle of a number of beautifully groomed exhibits parading in the rings at a dog show may fire the spectator with a desire to breed similar specimens good enough to win top honours in ring competition. In some cases the onus of breeding and rearing a litter may be thrust on an unwilling owner by a bitch straying from home while in season to form a misalliance with a mate of her own choosing. But whatever the reason and whether the object is the production of attractive pets or the breeding of show-quality stock, certain principles must be observed if the puppies are to be healthy and the mother brought safely through her ordeal.

The breeder who seeks to win distinction as an exhibitor, or who hopes to establish a successful strain of potential winners, must keep the ideal as depicted by the official breed standard clearly in mind and strive patiently to produce stock which approaches it more closely in each succeeding generation. For those who take up dog breeding for fun or with the object of disposing of their puppies as pets, such considerations may not be so important, but the desire to breed strong, healthy, intelligent puppies free from hereditary weakness, either physical or temperamental, will be equally strong. In this sense they, too, must breed to an ideal and they will succeed or fail in their aims according to whether they take trouble to understand and apply the basic laws which govern canine reproduction in all its phases.

Unfortunately, a novice breeder who sets out with high hopes and enthusiasm is sometimes sadly disappointed when the litter arrives. This result is almost inevitable if the method adopted is to acquire a bitch at random and to mate her to the first good-looking dog that happens to be readily available. The breeding of pedigree stock can never be raised to the status of an exact science, but a thoughtful breeder should be able to forecast with reasonable confidence what to expect from any carefully planned mating. Until comparatively recently livestock breeders had to rely on rule of thumb methods, plus whatever could be gleaned from intelligent observation, experience and common sense. Today things are different. The laws which govern heredity are pretty well understood and there is no longer any reason why the production of sound, typical, high-quality stock in any breed should be thought to depend on the 'luck of the dip'.

When we mate two animals we do so in the hope that certain desired qualities or characters will be transmitted by one or both of them to their offspring. In all serious breeding operations we set out to control the hereditary make-up of the puppies in the litters produced. If a bitch is weak in some point the obvious course is to try to offset that failing by putting her to a dog which is especially good in that respect, in the hope that the sire's influence will correct the maternal fault in the puppies. Unfortunately this system does not always work out as expected.

The idea that the good points shown by an animal depend on the characteristics shown by one or both of its parents has probably been responsible for more disappointments in breeding than any other fallacy. It is based on the assumption that the physical characters of sire and dam are passed on as such to their progeny—that like will produce like. That this is not so is clearly proved by the fact that a red puppy may have two black parents, a long-coated youngster may be born to two smooths, or a dog with drop ears come from parents in both of which the ears are erect.

Many breeders still appear to believe that genetics, the science that deals with the study of heredity, is so obscure and technical as to be beyond the comprehension of anyone but a specialist. This is very far from the truth. The basic principles, as they apply to the breeding of dogs, are quite simple and straightforward. A puppy originates in the union of two sex-cells, one contributed by each parent. It follows, therefore, that every characteristic it possesses must come from one or the other of these parental cells. According to genetic theory each innate character or point possessed by an individual is presented in the fertilised egg-cell by an ultramicroscopic particle called a gene. The development of black pigment in a dog's coat is due to the presence of one kind of gene, whereas the development of brown or red coat colour arises from the presence of another.

Similarly, long or short hair, differences in the shape and proportion of head, legs, ears, tail, or variations in temperament, resistance to certain types of diseases, keen or poor scent discrimination, or any of the features or traits that go to the making of an individual, represent visual expressions of the presence or absence of various genes and gene combinations.

The gene may be said to be the vital unit in heredity. What a puppy inherits is not the physical or mental characteristics of its parents, but genes which, in suitable environmental conditions, will cause certain qualities to develop, and these may or may not be similar to those shown by one or both of its parents.

The male and female germ cells which come together in fertilisation each carry a complete set of genes, so that a puppy receives one gene for every characteristic appropriate to its breed from each parent. Its body cells will, therefore, contain two of each kind of gene. On reaching maturity it will itself produce sex or germ cells—sperms if a dog and ova or egg-cells if a bitch. But in these cells the genes in each pair separate, so that a germ cell contains but one of each kind of gene. Thus, each of the body cells of a dog carries a double dose, whereas each of its germ cells carries only a single dose of each kind of gene. When a male and female germ cell unite during mating the numerical position is restored, half the number of genes which contribute to the genetical make-up of the resulting puppy coming from the sire and half from the dam. This may sound rather complicated, but a simple example may help to make it clear.

If we mate a brindle Boxer dog to a red bitch of the same breed, each being pure bred for its own colour, each of their puppies will receive one gene for brindle colour from its sire and one gene for red colour from its dam. All the body cells will, therefore, carry both genes. In appearance these puppies will be brindle, because the gene which determines the development of that colour inhibits the visual expression of red. Brindle is, for this reason, said to be dominant to red, which is recessive. But though puppies bred in this way will resemble their sire in colour, they may give quite different results if later they are used for breeding. All the germ cells produced by their sire carry genes for the brindle colour, but his offspring from a red bitch will produce germ cells of two types —one kind carrying the gene for brindle and the other carrying the gene for red. If a dog from this litter is, in turn, mated to a red bitch, some of her ova may be fertilised by sperms carrying the brindle gene and others by sperms carrying the red gene. In the former case the resulting puppies will be brindle (that colour being dominant and masking the presence of the red factor) while in the latter case they will be red. The chances of the ova available at the time of the mating being fertilised by a brindle- or a red-bearing sperm are equal, so that the theoretical expectation is that half the litter will be brindle and half red. If, however, we put one of the dogs from our first litter to a pure-bred brindle bitch we should expect to get a whole litter of brindles, for all the bitch's germ cells will carry the brindle genes and whether they unite with a brindle-bearing or a red-bearing sperm cell the dominant brindle colour will be shown by the puppy.

Were we to mate a dog and bitch from our first litter together, the results would be different. Both carry genes for both brindle and red. Each will, therefore, produce two types of germ cells, and there will be an equal likelihood of their sex-cells combining in any of four ways. A brindle-bearing sperm may unite with a brindle- or with a red-bearing ovum, or a red-bearing ovum may be fertilised either by a brindle- or a red-bearing sperm. If we use the letter B to indicate brindle and R to indicate red, we may express the possible combinations thus:

B × B
(sperm) (ovum)

B × R
(sperm) (ovum)

R × B
(sperm) (ovum)

R × R
(sperm) (ovum)

Puppies developing from any of the first three unions will be brindle, but any developing from the fourth (RR) will be red. Of the brindles one will be pure-bred for its own colour (BB), whereas the other two, (BR and RB), though showing the brindle colour, will carry the factor for red and will pass it on to a proportion of their progeny.

It is most important that a breeder who wishes to achieve lasting success in the production of high quality stock should clearly understand the meaning of the terms 'dominant' and 'recessive' in the genetic sense. A dog may show a dominant characteristic yet carry the recessive gene in its hereditary make-up; but any animal that shows a recessive characteristic must be genetically pure for that particular point. The mating of two individuals each showing a dominant trait may produce offspring showing the recessive condition, but two animals which show a recessive quality can never produce young which show the opposite dominant feature. Though we may breed red progeny from two brindle Boxers, we cannot breed a brindle puppy from two red parents.

It is impossible to give a list of the various canine characters that are dominant and to contrast them with those that are recessive. A character may be dominant to another character in one breed but recessive to it in another. For example, red is dominant to black and tan in the Dachshund but is recessive to black and tan in the Gordon Setter. A long foreface is dominant to short foreface in most dogs, but recessive in the bull-breeds. In general, it may be said that in pedigree stock those qualities that are regarded as desirable points are dominant to the reverse qualities which are regarded as faults. This has a very important bearing on the selection of breeding stock. Two animals which show the same fault should never be mated, since all their offsprings are almost certain to possess that fault, possible in a greater degree than their parents. On the other hand, if a bitch possessing some particular fault, such as a light eye or overshot jaw, is put to a dog which is not only himself perfect in these points but is known to come from a line of ancestors equally free from the blemish, all the puppies may be correct in eye colour or mouth formation. All will have inherited the dominant genes from their sire, which prevents the recessive condition of their dam from developing.It should be realised, however, that, though the fault in question has been 'corrected' in this generation, the puppies carry genes for the defect, inherited from their mother, and will be likely to sire or bear a proportion of faulty offspring if unwisely mated.

From what has been said it should be clear that in choosing a mate for a bitch the beginner should not be guided solely by outward appearances, or even by a dog's show record. Steps should also be taken to see that he comes from a line or strain that is free from any grave hereditary defect or weakness. This necessitates the examination of pedigrees and the acquisition of sufficient breed knowledge to enable the significance of such documents to be understood.

The surest way is to see as many of the dog's progeny as possible and to ascertain that no one fault occurs in a considerable proportion of his puppies. Remember that a recessive fault can only appear if the animal that shows it carries a double dose of the genes for that defect, which means that it must have inherited one dose from each of its parents. One of the first lessons a breeder should learn is never to breed from a bad dog with a good pedigree, or from a good dog with a bad pedigree.

CHAPTER 2

BREEDING THEORIES

THERE ARE few subjects which breeders discuss more often or with greater fervour than the part inbreeding can play in the improvement of type in pedigree dogs. The opinions expressed as regards the value or dangers of inbreeding as compared with line breeding, outcrossing and so on, show the widest divergencies. Some breeders look upon the system as representing an evil to be avoided at all costs, contending that it must bring disaster and ruin in its wake. Others claim that it is the only sure road to success for those whose aim it is to build up a strain which can be relied on to breed true for the breed points required. It is, however, equally illogical to suppose that in itself inbreeding is either a malignant force or a sovereign remedy for all the difficulties which lie in the breeder's path. Inbreeding is simply a means of sorting out the virtues and faults inherent in a strain or family. Whether its results are good or bad depends entirely on the type of the stock that is subjected to its influence and the care with which it is applied.

Although such words as inbreeding, line breeding and out breeding are in constant use in discussions on doggy matters, the terms are often used very loosely and frequently misunderstood. In the widest sense inbreeding consists in the inter-mating of relatives, and it is virtually impossible to breed pedigree stock of any kind without having recourse to it. As a rule, however, the term is used in a more restricted sense: to indicate the mating of such close relatives as mother and son, sire and daughter or brother and sister. The breeding together of more distantly related individuals such as cousins, uncle and niece, half brother and half sister, and so on, is referred to as line breeding. Many people who are strongly opposed to inbreeding are great advocates of line-breeding, yet there is no essential difference between the two. Line-breeding is merely a mild, or less intense, form of inbreeding.

In the previous chapter it was explained that genetically most of the points we seek to obtain in show stock are represented by dominant genes, while the unwanted characteristics, which we call faults, are produced by recessive genes. The ideal aimed at is to produce an animal which carries all the dominant genes in duplicate. Such a dog will not only approach its breed standard very closely itself but will pass on all its own good points to all its offspring. In efforts to breed to that ideal it is clearly necessary to select for mating a dog and bitch each typical for all essential breed qualities and carrying as many dominant genes as possible. That is, to bring together two animals that are genetically similar. The greater their genetic similarity the closer their progeny may be expected to resemble them.

In any breed of dogs two near relatives are likely to have more genes in common than are two unrelated individuals, and the closer their relationship the more alike genetically they are likely to be. The most direct method of producing genetic purity in a strain is, therefore, by inbreeding. But it must be remembered that genetic purity applies to faults as well as to virtues. Inbreeding will fix both good and bad points and will bring to light any weakness or defect which may be dormant in the parents. The first visual results of inbreeding may, therefore, be disappointing.

Litters born to an inbred mating may show some, possibly many, faults which were not apparent in either of the parents, but the genes for the development of those defects must have been carried by both sire and dam. Inbreeding cannot create either good or bad points. It can only make visible what is present, though hidden, in the animals that are mated.

It is a common fallacy to suppose that such failings as loss of vigour, weak pigmentation, impotence, sterility, susceptibility to infection, mental degeneration, loss of size or bad temperament can originate through inbreeding. If these, or any other defects appear in inbred stock it is because the parents carry the hereditary factors responsible for these conditions. The emergence of faults through the coming together of recessive genes can, of course, occur in litters bred from unrelated parents, but inbreeding certainly increases the risk.

Any characteristic, whether physical or mental, can be fixed in, or eliminated from, a strain by inbreeding. Physical or constitutional strength, fertility, fearlessness, size or high intelligence

Black and tan Cavalier puppies: bred by Mrs. Martin

Colour photos by Anne Cumbers

Smooth Fox Terrier puppy on good rations at the Pitlea kennels

Cavalier puppies: owned by Mrs. Rampton

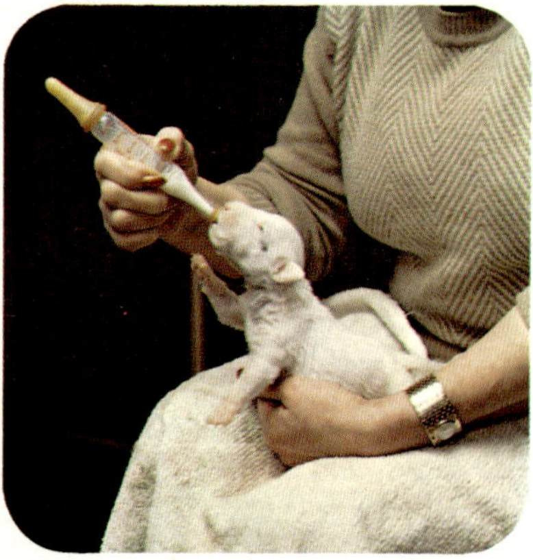

Hand rearing a Bull Terrier puppy: owner Mrs. Howard Williams

Ruby Cavalier puppies: owned by Mrs. Rampton

Weimaraner puppies: bred by Mrs. Veasey

Welsh Corgi bitch cleaning up a puppy: breeder Mrs. Parsons

Beagle bitch with newly born litter at the Crestamere kennels

and trainability may be inbred into a strain as surely as may such points as length of head, ear shape, eye-colour or coat texture. This fact is very apt to be ignored by those who seem to regard inbreeding as being inevitably associated with degeneration.

If the early results of inbreeding are disappointing the remedy is not to go over to outcrossing, but to continue to inbreed, with drastic weeding out of all faulty progeny as it appears. The main reason breeders who have only slight experience of inbreeding often decry it, is that they have failed to persevere long enough for the benefits which might have been derived from it to become apparent, or because they have not been ruthless enough in discarding all faulty or weakly puppies in the litters bred. If rigorous culling is practised in the early stages inbred stock will become increasingly more uniform both in appearance and genetically in later generations, so that a true breeding line of high quality, typical animals may be established.

It is useless to embark on a programme of inbreeding with chance-bred or mediocre stock. At every mating the animals chosen must be of high quality and free from any serious hereditary defects. Unless material of this calibre is available, efforts should be concentrated on building up a stock of sound, typical individuals by outcrossing, line-breeding and selection. The object of inbreeding is to produce a strain of animals all conforming closely to a desired pattern. The longer inbreeding is continued the more alike its products will become. In time it will be effective in fixing all the qualities inherent in a strain, both good and bad. If selection is applied with care and within wide enough limits in each generation, only the good points will be stabilised, but if faults are overlooked or ignored in the animals bred from, they, too, will be fixed in the strain and further inbreeding will cause deterioration.

In line-breeding the mated animals are less closely related, so that the resemblance of offspring to parents will probably be less strongly marked than in closely inbred stock. Genetic purity and physical uniformity will also take longer to achieve. But, though it is slower in fixing desirable qualities than inbreeding, line breeding is also less likely to expose faults. For that reason, where immediate results are of more importance than the ultimate establishing of a genuine true-breeding strain, it may be considered preferable and safer than inbreeding. It should, however, be understood that anything which may be gained through line-breeding may be obtained more quickly and more directly by inbreeding. The point to bear in mind is that the higher the general quality of a strain the closer it may be inbred without ill-effects, always providing that precautions are taken to weed out every puppy which fails to come up to a required standard.

To attempt to initiate a programme of inbreeding with inferior stock, or to continue with it when a fault shows signs of becoming fixed in the strain, is to court certain disaster.

An outcross—that is, the breeding together of two unrelated animals —should only be made for a special purpose. The belief that a change of blood must in all cases be salutary after inbreeding has been practised for a few generations is mistaken. If, through lack of care in selection or from other causes, a recessive fault becomes widespread in a strain, it may be necessary to resort to an outcross in order to bring in the dominant gene to correct it. The snag is that, however carefully the animal to be used as an outcross is chosen, he is almost certain to bring in not only the genes desired but other factors that are not wanted. He will probably be genetically impure for several of the qualities for which a high degree of genetic purity has been established in the line into which he is to be crossed, so that certain recessive genes will be passed on to any progeny sired by him. An outcross should be regarded as an experiment and in a well-established strain should not be made without good reason.

There are times when outcrossing may be imperative, as when a fault or weakness occurs repeatedly in members of a certain family or strain, but every effort should be made to see that the animal used brings in as few alien traits or genetic impurities as possible. The best way to ensure this is to try to find an individual which, though not closely related, carries some of the same foundation blood lines as the strain with which it is to be crossed. In a small or numerically weak breed that may not be feasible but in the more popular varieties a breeder resorting to indirect line-breeding, as opposed to inbreeding in the restricted sense, may be able to obtain the desired results with less risk than by a more drastic outcross.

Having made an outcross the next step is to breed back strongly to the original line. Except in very exceptional circumstances this is the only safe course to follow, once the purpose of outcrossing has been achieved. Only in this way can the genetic purity previously established in a valuable strain be maintained.

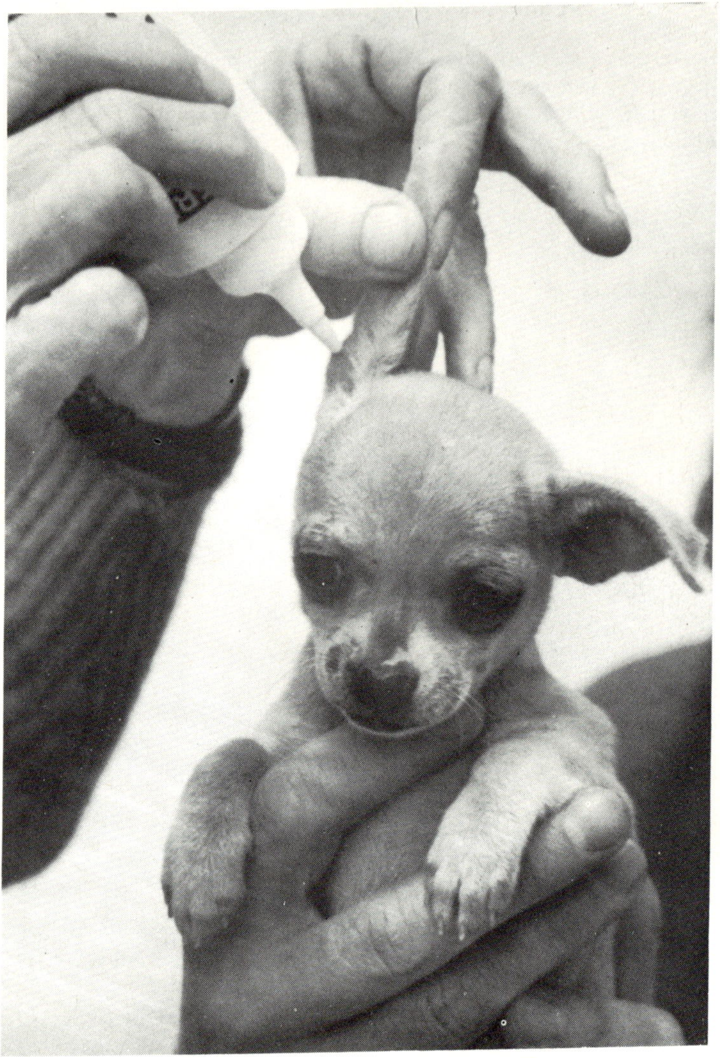

Two pairs of hands are better than one when medical attention has to be given to a young animal. Make sure the puppy is properly supported with one hand under the bottom, and the other under the chest.

CHAPTER 3

YOUR FIRST BITCH

MANY PEOPLE become dog breeders almost by accident; in some cases, perhaps, against their better judgement! Ofen the owner of a bitch, bought originally as a puppy for a pet, later feels strongly tempted to show her or breed a litter from her. Then arises the question, Is my bitch good enough to show, or is she likely to breed worthwhile puppies? To the first question the answer is probably No. Puppies sold as pets are not usually of show quality—that is why they are offered at pet prices, though there are, of course, exceptions to this rule. The answer to the second question may be more difficult to find.

When considering the potential breeding value of a bitch one must be guided by both her appearance and her pedigree. A bitch of the pet class may have a fairly good pedigree, come from sound stock, leave nothing to be desired in temperament and health, but, judged by show standards, her physical conformation will probably leave a good deal to be desired. From the point of view of show competition she may be of very mediocre quality and have certain definite faults.

The best course for the owner of a bitch of this kind who aspires to become a successful breeder is to try to obtain, or compile from such information as can be collected, an extended pedigree covering at least five or six generations. A careful study of this will indicate the best ancestors in her lineage and the blood lines they represent. The next step is to decide, as far as may be possible—and it is surprising how much information can be gleaned by patient and tactful enquiry—from which of these lines her most serious or obvious faults come. Should it be found that her failings may be traced to a definite line in her breeding, and that another line in her descent is free from the defects, the obvious course is to breed away from the faulty line but back to the best section of her pedigree, by mating her to a first class representative of that strain. He may be an uncle, cousin, of some kind or even a half brother. It may be, however, that investigation shows that the pedigree includes no really significant line that is wholly free from the inherent blemishes which it is wished to avoid. In that case recourse must be had to an outcross.

In either case the choice of the dog for this first mating is of vital importance. The stud selected must be a worthy representative of a family of line on which the prospective breeder is prepared to pin his faith and future hopes, because matings made in subsequent generations must be along the same line and should be as close as may be practicable. How good the first litter is must depend largely on the degree of genetical purity present in the sire; that is, on the extent to which he is doubly dominant in respect of these points in which the bitch fails and for which she must be assumed to be recessive.

From the resulting litter the best bitch should be selected and mated back to her sire's line. Again the greatest care must be taken in choosing the most suitable mate available; suitability being judged not merely by appearance, but also by the dog's breeding and stud record. When the litter arrives the best of the bitches should be retained and in due course mated on the lines already suggested. If this procedure is followed consistently and intelligently, careful thought being given in each generation to the selection of the stud dog used and to the picking of the best bitch in each litter from which to breed, the foundation of a reliable breeding strain may be laid in four or five generations. This does not mean that no show specimens will be produced before then. It may well be that in the first or second litters bred, one or more good winners will appear, but the stabilising of the desired type and the fixing of the genetic factors on which satisfactory breeding results depend, can hardly be achieved in less than about five generations.

When setting out to buy a bitch with which it is hoped to found a successful kennel, remember that both partners to a mating contribute equally to the making of the resulting offspring. Good looks in a bitch wanted for breeding purposes are valueless unless they go with good breeding. In the past much was written on the question of whether the sire or the dam has the greater influence on the shape and constitution of their progeny. As a rule the sire was held to be the more potent parent, but some breeders urged the over-riding importance of the bitch, believing that the dam was responsible for at least sixty per cent of any good qualities the members of the litter might possess. By some it was stated that while size, head and coat properties come from the sire, the dam transmits general body shape and temperament. A study of genetics makes it abundantly clear that all such theories are groundless.

Each parent contributes equally to the genetic make-up of a puppy. Good and bad points, or rather the genes that control them, may be passed on by either sire or dam. No characteristic, whether head shape, size, coat length, eye-colour or any other is transmitted exclusively by one parent. But, though the sire and dam are of equal importance in determining the genetic constitution of their offspring, the dam is pre-eminent in providing the conditions in which the young organisms will develop until ready to be born, and from then until they are weaned in maintaining the food supply.

When choosing a bitch it is of first importance to consider not only her actual appearance but to ensure, as far an may be possible, that she is of sound constitution, free from sexual or other abnormalities, and comes from hardy fertile stock. Certain physical traits should be looked for, including good bone and ample depth and breadth of ribbing. The amount of depth and width desired varies, of course, in different breeds, but flat-sided, shallow-chested bitches are to be avoided. The loin, too, should be reasonably broad, and rather more length in this region than would be approved in a dog should not be counted as a fault. A narrow, short, or constricted pelvis is most undesirable, for a bitch so constructed is almost certain to have difficulty in whelping. If the novice buyer finds it difficult to judge the width of the pelvis, the bitch should be watched from the rear as she moves. If the hind legs move, as they should, perpendicularly from hip joint to foot, and parallel to one another, the distance between the hocks will give a good indication of the width of the pelvis. A bitch which goes rather wide behind is to be preferred to one which goes too close.

If it is proposed to purchase a young adult bitch it is advisable to make enquiries as to whether she has been in season. Though bitches vary widely as regards the age at which they experience their first heat, a bitch that does not come in season for the first time until long after her first birthday, or has infrequent or irregular periods, *may* breed successfully, but her condition may be symptomatic of some disturbance or failing in some part of her sexual physiology which is likely to make her of dubious value as a brood.

Shy and timid bitches are best avoided. It is often said that the temperament of a shy bitch improves after she has had a litter, but that is not always the case. If the shyness or timidity is of genetic origin, as it often is, it may be passed on to her puppies. A timorous bitch may turn out to be a bad mother, either becoming hysterical at whelping time and refusing to tend or nurse her puppies, or being so possessive as to be difficult to manage when her family arrives. The type of bitch to look for is an alert but mentally stable animal which shows no physical or temperamental weakness or abnormality.

A soft, lethargic bitch which tends to put on too much weight on a normal diet is not recommended. Such a bitch is often irregular in her periods of heat and may be a lazy whelper. During pregnancy she may tend to use the food supplied mainly for her own benefit, so that she becomes increasingly corpulent while her whelps are inadequately nourished.

As regards choosing a potential brood bitch by her outward physical qualities, opinions among breeders have always been sharply divided as to whether a mediocre bitch that shows few or no serious faults is to be preferred to one in which excellence in certain points is accompanied by one or two definite faults. My own preference is for a bitch of the latter kind, as I believe she may be relied on to transmit something of positive value to any puppies she may bear. If care is taken to mate her to a dog which from his stud record may reasonably be thought to be genetically pure for the dominant characteristics in which she is wanting, the offspring are likely to possess fewer failings than would the progeny of a mediocre bitch with no serious fault.

It is not suggested that worthwhile show dogs can only be bred from a bitch which is capable of winning in good company. Most experienced breeders could cite many examples of successful exhibits which have come from dams that it would be a waste of time to show. But though these bitches have been wanting in certain of the qualities looked for in ring competition, they have, nevertheless, been good as regards some of the primary characteristics of their breed.

A bitch which lacks any sort of distinction, though showing no grave fault, cannot be regarded as a likely foundation on which a winner-producing strain may be built. She may be well-bred, as judged by the number of high sounding names included in her pedigree, but she probably carries genes for the worst of the qualities inherent in the lines which have contributed to her ancestry, and cannot transmit to any of her descendants those hereditary factors which go to the making of outstanding show type.

Bloodhound puppies aged 5 weeks, bred by Mr. and Mrs Porter, "Sherlock", Stalisfield, Kent.

CHAPTER 4

THE BITCH IN SEASON

As a general rule a bitch comes into season, or on heat, every six or seven months. But this is a rule to which there are many exceptions. The first heat may occur at any time after the age of about four months, or be delayed until a bitch is well over twelve months old. Bitches of the smaller breeds tend to come in season earlier and more often than those of the larger breeds, but this is not invariably the case. Some foreign breeds, like the Basenji and Finnish Spitz, when first imported came on heat only once a year, but now that they have been domiciled and bred in this country for several years, owing no doubt to our more clement climate and to generous feeding, many of the bitches have a bi-annual breeding cycle.

The length of time which elapses between the first and subsequent heats may vary from four to twelve months or more. In this respect every bitch seems to be a law to herself. A young, highly sexed bitch may have successive heats at intervals of a few months as long as she remains unmated, but after she has had a litter her seasons may be normally spaced. If a bitch is not bred from until she is over three years old her heats may tend to become more infrequent or irregular. Severe illness may delay the onset of heat and the duration of the condition may vary with the seasons; being shorter in winter than in summer.

The first indication that heat is imminent is the swelling of the external genital parts, accompanied by a slight, colourless discharge. A few days later the discharge becomes reddish owing to the presence of blood in the mucus. The coloured discharge usually continues for from three to eight days, after which it becomes colourless and diminishes in quantity. This is the normal sequence of events. In exceptional cases the whole period may pass without any sign of a coloured discharge. Even when it occurs the uterine bleeding varies both in severity and duration. In some bitches the flow is fairly copious and continues for a week or more, while in others it is hardly noticeable and is limited to a day or two. The amount of this discharge bears no relationship to fecundity. A bitch which never shows colour at any stage in her heat may bear as large litters and prove as reliable as a brood as one in which there is a copious reddish discharge.

The occurrence of a colourless heat may be the explanation when a bitch produces a litter despite her owner's conviction that is it impossible for a mating to have taken place, as the bitch was never in contact with a dog at any time during her season. The probability is that in the absence of the expected 'colour' the owner failed to realise the bitch's condition until heat was far advanced, by which time a mating had already occurred.

A bitch generally remains on heat for about three weeks, though, excetionally, the period may be considerably longer. Her season may be divided into three phases. The first is the preliminary phase during which certain changes occur in the uterus, or womb, in preparation for the role that organ will play if conception is effected. This phase usually lasts from seven to nine days and is marked by a more or less copious discharge. The second, or secretory, phase extends from about the eighth to the fifteenth day. It is during this phase that ripe egg-cells or ova, are released from the ovaries and pass to the openings of the oviducts, where they remain until fertilised or, if the bitch is unmated, until the termination of her heat, when they disintegrate. The third, or recuperative, phase lasts about a week and completes the cycle.

Some bitches are willing to mate at almost any time in the course of their heat, but the majority are most eager to do so during the middle phase. Though fruitful mating is not necessarily limited to this phase, conception is more likely to occur, and a larger litter produced, if union is effected at this time. From the tenth to the fourteenth day from the onset of heat is normally the best for service. Late rather than early mating is advisable, in order to ensure that the full number of ripe ova shall be available for fertilisation in the oviducts. If a bitch is mated too early the sperms, or male germ cells, may have lost their vitality before the full complement of ova has been shed from the ovary: while if service is too long delayed the ova may have become inert by the time the sperms reach them.

A bitch, having passed through what appears to be a normal

heat, may again come in season after the lapse of a few weeks. When this occurs the first must be assumed to have been what is known as a false heat, or pseudo-oestrum. The second is the true heat. If the bitch was mated during the first period she will 'miss'—that is, conception will not have occurred. If a litter is desired she should be mated again at the appropriate phase of her second heat.

While she is in season a bitch must, of course, be carefully secluded to prevent any possibility of a misalliance. She should be exercised at such times and in such places as to be unlikely to attract the interest of wandering dogs. One of the preparations especially made to mask the natural scent, dabbed on the hind-quarters, may be used with advantage, or suitable pills or tablets may be given for the purpose of preventing stray dogs collecting about the house or kennel at this time.

It is almost inevitable that during the period of heat a bitch will get rather less than her usual amount of exercise. Special care should be taken to ensure that she does not become constipated, and attention given to her diet. She should be kept warm and dry, and prevented from sitting or lying about in cold winds or on damp ground. Neglect of these precautions may lead to metritis, or inflammation of the womb. The first signs of this disorder are loss of appetite and a sharp rise in temperature. The abdomen becomes distended and tender and, there is a pinkish, offensive discharge from the vagina. Unless appropriate measures are taken the accumulated pus may break through the walls of the uterus and death from peritonitis supervene. Hot fomentations to the abdomen may bring relief in the initial stages and the vagina should be syringed freely and often with warm boric solution. Veterinary assistance should be obtained as soon as possible.

Should it be considered necessary to bath a bitch while she is in season, great care should be taken to dry her thoroughly in a warm place before she is allowed to lie down or is put into an out-door kennel. The same precautions must be observed if she comes home wet from exercise.

A litter of Mallinois puppies.

CHAPTER 5

THE UNWANTED SEASON

THERE ARE many occasions when it is extremely inconvenient for a bitch to come into season, and now, with the aid of modern science, it is possible to either delay the onset of an unwanted season, or to prevent it altogether.

Delaying the season can be achieved by administering Megestrol Acetate tablets which are supplied through the Vet. The tablets must be given before the season actually begins, and can be given for a period of up to forty days, and even longer in a smaller dosage. As these need to be given about 14 days before the expected onset, it is necessary to advise your Vet of your intentions, ask him if there is any special reason why he does not recommend their use in the case of your bitch, and, all being well, he will give you the required number of tablets.

If you have left things a little late, the manufacturers state that they prefer the tablets to be given fourteen days before, but they can be given seven days before. However, it is not wise to use the tablets for more than one course in any six months.

After your bitch has been on this course of tablets, it will be impossible for anyone to tell you when she will next come into season. In the average case, it can be expected about 3 months later, but in other cases it may be three weeks, or twenty-six weeks, but seldom longer.

The same tablets can be given immediately the season begins, but in this case they are a stronger dosage, and the course lasts 8 days. The signs of the season usually disappear in two to three days, but again it cannot be said with any certainty when the bitch will next come into season, but it should be expected about six weeks earlier than usual.

The oral administration of this synthetic hormone allows much more control over the duration of the effect of its usage, and consequently it is the wisest form of administration if the bitch concerned is one which you wish to use for breeding at a later date.

By the time the next season comes around, it should have cleared from the body and normal conception should be achieved.

The other method of preventing the unwanted season is by an injection, one month before the onset of the season.

As this method means a large dosage being administered at one time, the length of time its affect will remain is dependent on the metabolism of the bitch, the placing of the injection itself, and such like. In consequence, although this method will certainly do away with the unwanted season, it is possible that it may do its work for longer than is desirable if a bitch is required for breeding. The return to the normal cycling may be six months later, but it is usually longer, the average time is eight to nine months but, be warned, it could be TWENTY-SIX MONTHS or more, and even then, the manufacturers do not advise mating on the next season.

If you have already used the injection method and are now quite ready to 'tear your hair out' by the foregoing—take heart, you have been told what could happen, not what will happen, and the following history may help to relieve your anxiety.

Peter Taylor of Vanyanic Keeshonds had a bitch called Vanyanic Red Witch of Rhinevale. Red Witch was mated and gave birth to ten puppies, nine of which lived.

Because she was coming into season when the family were going on holiday, and she was one of the family, she was given the injection. Eight months later she came into season and was mated. Again she gave birth to a large litter of eleven puppies, one of which was stillborn, and another faded, so once again nine lived. In this litter were three good show dogs, Vanyanic Boy Blue, Vanyanic Pinnochio, and Vanyanic Peter Pan. At a later date, Red Witch was given the eight day course of pills and came into season three months later, when she was mated. On this occasion she again reared nine puppies, one of which Vanyanic Double Dutch who can be seen as a baby with his big brother Vanyanic Boy Blue in the Photograph opposite. Double Dutch went best of breed at Maidstone at the age of 9 months in November 1974.

The litters were all fairly evenly spread over the sexes; there was nothing different about any of the three whelpings, nor were there any malformed pups.

Vanyanic Boy Blue with brother—both born after use of megestrol acetate

THIRD PRIZE
THIRD PRIZE
2ND PRIZE Vetzyme
CRUFTS
DOG
FIRST PRIZE
SHOW
OLYMPIA 1974
2ND PRIZE Vetzyme
1ST PRIZE Vetzyme
V.H.C.
RESERVE
3RD PRIZE

Chesapeek Bay Retriever enjoying life with her babies

CHAPTER 6

MATING

HAVING CHOSEN the dog to which the bitch is to be mated, the next step is to inform his owner of your intention, at the same time telling him when the bitch is expected to be ready. Immediately the first signs of her coming in heat appear, advise the dog's owner and arrange the time of arrival at the kennel. This is important, as successful studs, especially in the more popular breeds, are often heavily booked and unless good notice is given it may be found impossible to get the bitch mated to the dog selected at the most favourable stage in the heat. If possible, accompany the bitch and be present at the mating. A long, lonely journey by rail in a travelling box is almost sure to upset a young bitch, making her bewildered and nervous, in which state she may be very unwilling to mate in unfamiliar surroundings and under the supervision of strangers. An unhurried excursion with a trusted human companion is a very different matter. This will leave her quite unperturbed and should she be at first disinclined to submit to the dog's advances, a little judicious coaxing and encouragement by her owner will usually quieten her. If circumstances make it necessary for the bitch to be sent by rail, let the owner of the dog know the route and the train by which she is to travel. Inform him, too, of her pet name and give particulars of any temperamental peculiarities she may have—whether she is nervous with other dogs, shy of strangers or children and so on—and of any special feeding fads, so that she may be made as comfortable as possible during her stay. Avoid worrying a sensitive bitch by rushing her about in a tearing hurry to get the mating over.

Arrange to arrive in good time, so that she may be exercised and rested before mating is attempted, and after union has been satisfactorily completed let her have at least half an hour's rest before setting out on her return journey. Neither dog nor bitch should be fed for some hours prior to mating, and both should be exercised before being brought together. If a bitch has to travel a long way home after being mated she should be given a light meal before her departure.

The actual mating should be effected in a secluded place where the pair are not likely to be worried or excited by outside noises or the intrusion of strangers or other dogs. The dog and bitch should be introduced quietly and cautiously, each being held on a lead. If the bitch seems unwilling to accept service, backing away from or snapping at the dog, she should be given a chance to get to know him in a run, in which the two may be kept close together and in full view of one another but separated by a wire partition. As soon as they seem to be friendly the dog may be put in with the bitch, but a watch must be kept on them in case of hostilities.

If a bitch resolutely refuses to have anything to do with the dog after half an hour or so, it is best to take her away and try her again after an interval of a few hours, or even to leave her for a day or two, before making another attempt. A maiden bitch may refuse to stand to a dog from fear or nervousness and it may be necessary to hold her firmly, with one hand on the collar and the other under her loins, to prevent her sitting down. With a strong bitch of one of the larger breeds it may take two people to keep her under proper control. The dog should be on a lead but restrained as little as possible. When mating has been accomplished the bitch must be prevented from moving or turning in efforts to throw the dog off.

Successful coition is normally followed by a tie. In the dog full erection occurs only after penetration, when the swollen base of the penis is held firmly by the contraction of the vulva. Conception may occur without a tie but is uncertain, for there is a risk that the seminal fluid may flow back through the external aperture of the vagina and be lost. Some bitches seem to be physically incapable of holding the dog. In such cases the dog should be prevented from dismounting and the pair held together for ten minutes. When the tie has been in operation for a minute or two the fore legs of the dog should be carefully lifted and placed on the ground on the right side of the bitch. Then the left hind leg should be lifted over the bitch's back, so that the pair stand tail to tail. A mated pair must on no account be left unattended while they are tied, or one or both may be injured either through the bitch sitting down or as a result of the dog indulging in violent movements.

The tie may last from ten minutes to an hour. Throughout this time the two animals must be kept still until natural release occurs.

Before taking or sending a maiden bitch to a stud dog it is well worth while to have her examined by a veterinary surgeon to see that there is nothing to impede normal mating. Many of the difficulties which novice owners experience when trying to get their bitches mated are due to the presence of membraneous or fibrous obstructions in some part of the vaginal passage. Such strictures may be quickly and easily broken down, but it is better to have this done a few days before the mating rather than to leave it until time and trouble have been wasted in fruitless efforts to bring about a satisfactory union.

It is wise to worm the bitch before the onset of the season if mating is intended, as this definitely does help to reduce the number of worms in the puppies. Years ago the worming of a dog was an ordeal for dog and owner, but nowadays the treatment is so safe and easy to administer that there can be no possible excuse for allowing a wormy bitch to have puppies, and possibly losing some in consequence. It is possible to worm the bitch after the mating has taken place, and this can safely be done up to a fortnight after the mating, for roundworm, but for any other worm it would be wise to seek veterinary advice.

At what age should a bitch be mated? This question is very difficult to answer in terms of years. Bitches of various breeds, and even individuals of the same breed, differ so much in size and the age at which they reach maturity that no hard and fast rule can be laid down. The advice often given to the novice to mate a bitch intended as a brood at her second heat is unreliable, since very wide variations occur both in the age at which the first heat is experienced and in the interval which elapses between it and the next season. The only satisfactory guide is physical development. No bitch should be bred from until she is fully grown and has the physique necessary to fit her for the ordeal of bearing and rearing a litter. It is inadvisable to mate a bitch until she is at least twelve months old. At that age it may be safe to breed from some of the smaller varieties but in larger breeds a further six, nine or twelve months may be required to bring full maturity.

Every effort should be made to get a bitch into hard, muscular condition as the time for mating draws near. It is better to have her on the lean than on the fat side. If a maiden bitch is fat at the time she is mated there will be little chance of getting rid of her surplus flesh during pregnancy, and corpulence is one of the most frequent causes of both missing and whelping troubles.

If a bitch is mated while still very young and undeveloped, her first litter is usually smaller than her later ones, because in immature animals the blood is deficient in the hormones responsible for full ovarian activity. This is another reason for refraining from breeding from a bitch until skeletal growth is completed. It is probable that her litter will be small and the strain imposed on her immature body is likely to arrest her further development and may spoil her for future breeding. On the other hand, a prospective brood should not be left unmated much beyond her third birthday. If she is she may have only two or three puppies, some of which may be so large as to make whelping so difficult or protracted as to endanger the dam's life.

The advisability of mating a bitch during the middle period of her heat has already been mentioned. In general, between the tenth and the fourteenth days is the time most likely to ensure conception and the birth of a full litter. An owner must, however, be guided in some degree by the bitch's behaviour. The old belief, which is still held by some breeders, that the sex of the puppies may be influenced by the stage in the heat at which mating is carried out is an irrational superstition. There is no known method whereby the sex of puppies can be controlled. The sex of each member of a litter is determined at the moment of fertilisation of the egg-cell from which it originates, and nothing the breeder can do will alter it.

Another much discussed question is whether it is advisable to have a bitch served twice to ensure her having a large litter. If the first mating is satisfactory and occurs at the proper time, a second is unnecessary and pointless. In normal coition several hundred million sperm cells are ejected by the dog, but only one is needed to fertilise an ovum. Every ripe egg-cell present in the genital tract of a bitch should, therefore, be fertilised at one mating. If, however, a mating occurs unduly early in a heat, before the full number of ova have been shed by the ovary, a second service may ensure the fertilisation of any egg-cells that have been released since the first took place.

The size of the litter is determined in the main by the bitch, unless the dog is sub-fertile or sterile. Several factors may cause or contribute to impaired fertility in the male. The germ cells may be of low vitality, so that they fail to penetrate the uterus to reach the ova or, having reached them, may be incapable of effecting fertilisation. Other things that may cause poor virility include under-feeding and over-use of a young dog or over-feeding and under-use of an older animal. A diet deficient in protein retards sperm production, as does lack of vitamins A, B and E. Close confinement and lack of exercise may be contributory causes. Certain generalised diseases which produce a feverish condition of the body, such as para-distemper, may induce temporary sterility, lasting from a few months to a year or more.

The question how often a stud dog may be used without loss of keenness and vigour cannot be answered categorically. Individual dogs vary greatly in the rate at which their sperm reserves become exhausted in successive ejaculations. A highly fertile dog may be able to serve two bitches a week through the year without any decline in his powers, whereas a dog of low fertility may be reliable only if used not more than once in two or three weeks.

A frequent cause of a bitch failing to be in whelp after what appears to have been a perfectly satisfactory mating is the acid reaction of the contents of the vagina. This destroys the sperm cells before they can reach the uterus, and thus prevents conception. The condition may be overcome by douching the vaginal passage with a lukewarm solution of bicarbonate of soda an hour or two prior to service. This treatment is simple and harmless and may be adopted as a precautionary measure before all matings, especially in the case of untried bitches and of those which have missed to previous matings.

Some time ago I was asked to advise the owner of a White West Highland Terrier bitch from which it was strongly desired to obtain a litter but which had been mated to proven stud dogs at four successive heats without result. This bitch had been under veterinary observation for some time and had had hormone injections and courses of vitamin E, but to no purpose. I suggested that, if it was decided to mate her again as a last resort, she should be douched with a dilute alkaline solution shortly before service.

This was done, with the result that she produced a litter of six puppies. She has recently been mated again, after douching, and is showing heavily in whelp.

CHAPTER 7

CARE OF THE PREGNANT BITCH

AFTER BEING mated a bitch should be allowed to follow her usual routine, both as regards food and exercise. Novice owners are apt to be over-anxious and make the mistake to treating the mother-to-be as an invalid. This is most unwise. It is quite unnecessary to increase a bitch's food allowance immediately she has been mated. Increased rations at this time can do nothing but harm. If she is in good condition the feeding routine to which she is accustomed should remain unaltered for the first five weeks.

In the early stages of pregnancy the nourishing of the coming family makes no considerable demands on the dam, and the amount of food she consumes has no direct influence on the growth of the embryo puppies. If a bitch is poorly fed at this time the developing young will absorb nourishment at the expense of the mother's tissues, so that even if the bitch loses weight from being inadequately fed her family will not necessarily suffer. This principle does not apply in the later stages of pregnancy. If the bitch is then underfed the growth of the unborn young will be arrested and deterioration or death may result. The weight and condition of a puppy at birth depends largely on the treatment of the dam during the last few weeks of pregnancy. After the fifth week her diet should be gradually supplemented by the addition of extra meat, fish, milk, eggs and other high protein foods. If as her time approaches she seems uncomfortable after a large meal, or disinclined to eat much at a time, two, three or even four meals of about equal size may be given, together with calcium.

Throughout the whole period of pregnancy over-feeding and under-exercising must be most carefully avoided. If a pregnant bitch puts on a lot of weight she is taking in more food than is required to satisfy her own and her family's needs. A lesson may be learnt by observing the ways of wild animals. A wild she-dog, wolf or jackal never puts on so much weight while carrying young as to impede her movements, and probably consumes less, rather than more, food than at other times. At full term she is active, lean and muscular—very different from the lethargic, fat, soft type of bitch which is so often the cause of anxiety and disappointment when due to whelp.

Plenty of exercise is essential and no restriction should be imposed on her freedom of movement until her increasing girth makes her awkward or incapable of enjoying long, brisk walks or energetic play. The longer she can be persuaded to follow a normal, active life the fitter she will be to stand up to the ordeal of whelping and the stronger will her puppies be. A bitch that is naturally lazy and shows an inclination to lie about as soon as her flanks begin to thicken, should be taken out and made to take sufficient exercise several times each day; not just turned out to wander round a garden for a few minutes now and again. But while active exercise should be encouraged, reasonable precautions must be taken in the last fortnight of pregnancy to see that the bitch does not injure herself by foolhardy actions. See that she has no chance to squeeze through narrow openings and do not allow her to jump up or down from any considerable height.

Most bitches tend to become quieter and more careful of themselves when pregnancy is well established, but others will continue to indulge in boisterous romps or tussles with kennel companions unless suitably controlled.

Reliable signs of pregnancy are not shown until the end of the fourth or fifth week, when a swelling of the flanks and a general rounding of the body may become apparent. Some bitches do not show their condition until the end of the sixth week. Much depends on the dam's physical build and the size of the coming litter. The appearance of the bitch is no true guide to the number of puppies she will produce. Some prolific bitches never get very big, while others which give early promise of having a numerous family actually give birth to only two or three puppies. By the end of the fifth week pregnancy may be indicated by an enlargement of the nipples and during the sixth week a veterinary sergeon may be able to confirm the presence of foetuses by palpitation.

When lifting a pregnant bitch never pick her up by the loose skin of the neck or by the elbows. Instead, place one hand under the chest and the other beneath the rump, so that she is raised in a horizontal position, while being securely and comfortably held. If she is too large or too heavy to be lifted in this way, she should be placed on a platform of some kind before being moved. If she is to be lifted on to a raised bench her forepaws should first be placed on the higher position and then the hind legs.

A novice owner may be perturbed to notice what appear to be symptoms of pregnancy in a bitch which has never been mated. The nipples may swell, the flanks increase in girth and milk be exuded in considerable quantities. This condition is due to what is referred to as false pregnancy, the causes of which are not fully understood. The symptoms usually become noticeable about the end of the fourth week following the termination of a heat, and may continue until the date on which the bitch would have whelped had she been mated. While in this condition a bitch may show special affection for her owner or be unusually demonstrative with her kennel companions. She may make determined efforts to make a bed in a quiet, secluded corner and generally behave to though about to whelp. The belief that bitches in which false pregnancy occurs are unlikely to be satisfactory for breeding is quite unfounded. On the contrary, they are usually strongly maternal and make excellent, prolific broods. The mistaken idea probably arises from confusing false pregnancy with another condition which often passes under that name but which is more correctly referred to as phantom pregnancy. This occurs in bitches which have been mated and become pregnant but which at full-term fail to produce puppies, although they have previously appeared to be heavy in whelp. In this case failure to give birth to a litter is due to the embryos having died at some stage in their development and been absorbed.

Pre-natal death may be caused by an unfavourable uterine environment. Anything that interferes with the nutrition, circulation or growing space of a foetus, or which exerts a disturbing influence on the mother, may bring about abortion, or result in the puppy being still-born. Among the environmental circumstances which most often cause abortion or premature labour are violent jars or blows, severe shock or strenuous exercise carried to the verge of exhaustion.

The death of a puppy in late pregnancy may induce premature labour, but some weedy type bitches fail to go full term for no assignable reason. The foetuses may be weakly and incapable of completing normal development but the possibility of a lethal genetic factor being involved cannot be ruled out.

There is no direct connection between false pregnancy and phantom pregnancy. The former affects only unmated bitches, whereas the latter can only occur in bitches which have been mated and got in whelp.

False pregnancy may be a source of annoyance and disappointment to an exhibitor, for it may, for a time, adversely affect a bitch's appearance and change her temperament, so that she is considerably handicapped in ring competition. Unfortunately, there is little the owner can do either to minimise the effects or to hasten the passing of the condition. The diet should be reduced and all food be fed dry. Except for drinking water, no fluids of any kind should be allowed. Plenty of brisk exercise is essential and the bowels should be kept working freely by small doses of castor oil or salts. The milk-glands should be dabbed several times daily with a 50 per cent dilution of methylated spirit. Unless the breasts become hard and congested the milk should not be drawn off, as this is likely to encourage secretion. Isolation of the bitch from kennel companions sometimes helps. She should, in any case, be kept away from a nursing bitch and from young puppies, as such contacts tend to prolong or exacerbate the trouble by exciting her maternal instincts.

CHAPTER 8

PREPARING FOR THE FAMILY

A FORTNIGHT before the bitch is due to whelp consideration should be given to the quarters she is to occupy during that critical time. The place chosen should be warm, dry, sufficiently commodious to enable her to move about in comfort without being unduly cramped, but snug and secluded. It should be well away from sight and sound of other dogs, and of tradesmen and chance visitors.

When whelping, and for a week after her litter is born, a bitch needs above all else a feeling of security and privacy, with freedom from all worry, noise or other distractions.

If possible she should be brought indoors and accommodated in a roomy box, placed out of the way in a corner of the kitchen or in a spare room so that she may be kept under observation and be given immediate attention should things go wrong or take an unexpected course. Should circumstances make it necessary for her to be in an outside kennel, a separate whelping chamber should be devised and a good sized box of suitable dimensions installed therein. The whelping box should be square and afford ample space for both the dam and her puppies. The length should be about equal to that of the bitch when stretched at full length. If it is rather larger so much the better (*see* Fig. 1).

A flange of wood a few inches deep fixed round the sides, a little lower than the height of the bitch's back when she is lying down, is a safeguard against any of the puppies being overlaid or otherwise injured by a nervous or clumsy mother.

It is a great advantage if an indoor whelping box is enclosed by solid wooden walls on three sides, with a barred or netted front, which can be opened when necessary, and a hinged top. This will enable the bitch to be confined when desirable, prevent outside interference and keep the puppies from falling out when they begin to scramble about. The actual shape and design may vary with the breed concerned. For toy and other small dogs suitable whelping

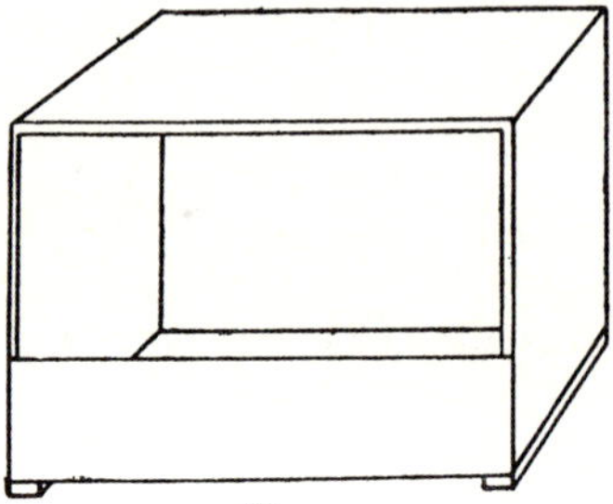

Fig. 1.

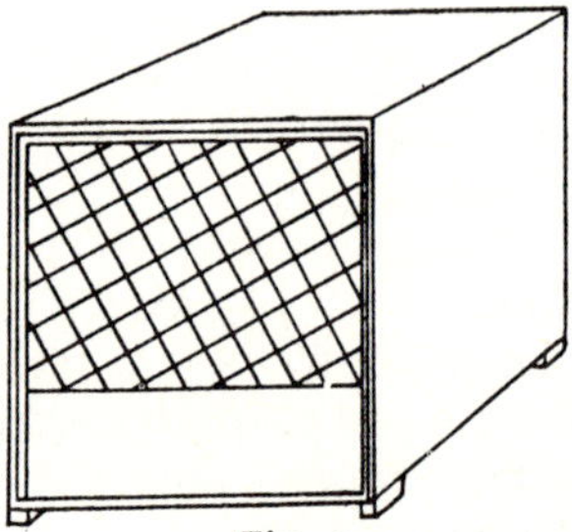

Fig. 2.

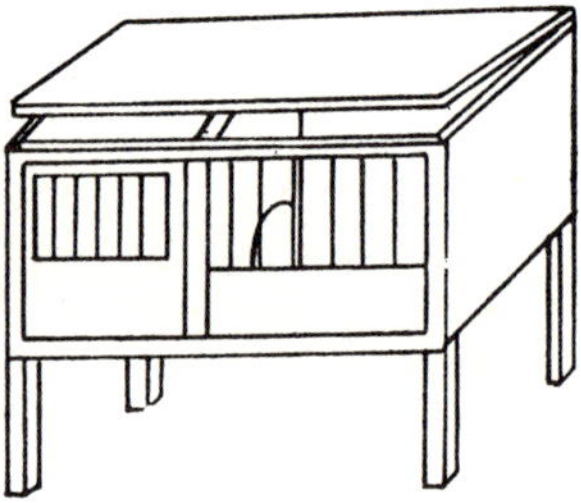

Fig. 3.

Fig. 1. *Open whelping box*
Fig. 2. *Closed whelping box with netted front (hinged)*
Fig. 3. *Whelping kennel for Toys (indoors)*
Fig. 4. *Whelping and sleeping box for use in outside kennel*

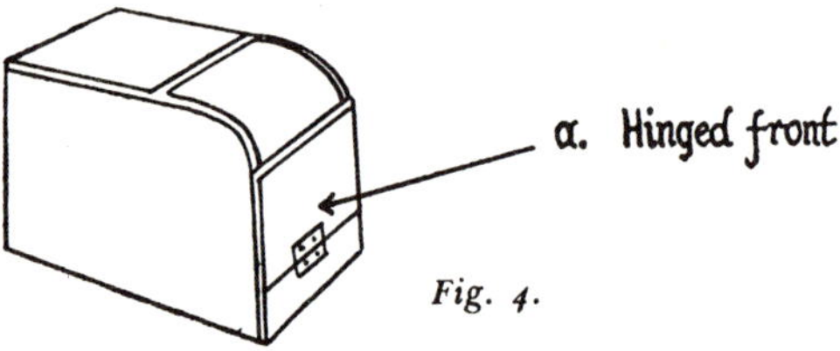

Fig. 4.

quarters may be arranged in an indoor kennel raised from the floor on short legs to make it easier to attend to the inmates and at the same time keep them well out of the way of draughts. Bitches prefer to whelp in conditions bearing some resemblance to the holes or caverns chosen for that purpose by their wild ancestors, and for the first two weeks puppies should be kept away from bright light. The whelping box should, therefore, be placed in an alcove or corner which is rather dimly lit. In an enclosed whelping box or kennel the light will be sufficiently dimmed, but it may be advisable to erect a temporary screen about an open box to keep it in semi-darkness.

The bitch should be introduced to her whelping quarters at least a week before her litter is expected, so that she may become familiar with them. Unless this is done she may resent being taken from her usual kennel or sleeping box and, when her time comes, make desperate efforts to get away from the unaccustomed surroundings to some secret retreat in which to have her family. A highly strung bitch may become quite panicky and, unless quietened and controlled, may, by her frenzied movements, injure either herself or her unborn puppies. To avoid any such difficulties make all preparations for settling her in her whelping accommodation in good time, so that she may be happily ensconced before the onset of that state of mental excitement and unrest which often precedes parturition, especially in a young bitch having her first litter.

The most hygienic method of whelping a bitch is to use a thick bed of newspapers. As the top sheets become soiled, they can be quickly removed, and, when the whelping is over, a completely fresh supply makes a clean fresh bed for mother and babies. The soiled paper can be easily burned and so there is no chance of the bedding harbouring unwanted parasites. Clean, cheap and trouble-free.

There are some people who prefer to bed pups down on blankets, but these have to be washed very frequently indeed, and a large supply of blankets is required if the area is to be kept really clean. Another reason for not using blankets is to avoid the possibility of a puppy becoming inadvertently trapped in the blanket and suffocated.

During the whelping, the temperature of the whelping area should be about 75 degrees F. It is therefore wise to give this matter some thought before the event.

One method which is widely used is to hang a heating lamp over the whelping box on a long piece of string. The height of the lamp affects the amount of heat in the box, and a double piece of stout string can be knotted at intervals allowing the lamp to be raised

GESTATION TABLE

Showing when your bitch is due to whelp

MATED JANUARY	DUE TO WHELP MARCH	MATED FEBRUARY	DUE TO WHELP APRIL	MATED MARCH	DUE TO WHELP MAY	MATED APRIL	DUE TO WHELP JUNE	MATED MAY	DUE TO WHELP JULY	MATED JUNE	DUE TO WHELP AUGUST	MATED JULY	DUE TO WHELP SEPTEMBER	MATED AUGUST	DUE TO WHELP OCTOBER	MATED SEPTEMBER	DUE TO WHELP NOVEMBER	MATED OCTOBER	DUE TO WHELP DECEMBER	MATED NOVEMBER	DUE TO WHELP JANUARY	MATED DECEMBER	DUE TO WHELP FEBRUARY
1	5	1	5	1	3	1	3	1	3	1	3	1	2	1	3	1	3	1	3	1	3	1	2
2	6	2	6	2	4	2	4	2	4	2	4	2	3	2	4	2	4	2	4	2	4	2	3
3	7	3	7	3	5	3	5	3	5	3	5	3	4	3	5	3	5	3	5	3	5	3	4
4	8	4	8	4	6	4	6	4	6	4	6	4	5	4	6	4	6	4	6	4	6	4	5
5	9	5	9	5	7	5	7	5	7	5	7	5	6	5	7	5	7	5	7	5	7	5	6
6	10	6	10	6	8	6	8	6	8	6	8	6	7	6	8	6	8	6	8	6	8	6	7
7	11	7	11	7	9	7	9	7	9	7	9	7	8	7	9	7	9	7	9	7	9	7	8
8	12	8	12	8	10	8	10	8	10	8	10	8	9	8	10	8	10	8	10	8	10	8	9
9	13	9	13	9	11	9	11	9	11	9	11	9	10	9	11	9	11	9	11	9	11	9	10
10	14	10	14	10	12	10	12	10	12	10	12	10	11	10	12	10	12	10	12	10	12	10	11
11	15	11	15	11	13	11	13	11	13	11	13	11	12	11	13	11	13	11	13	11	13	11	12
12	16	12	16	12	14	12	14	12	14	12	14	12	13	12	14	12	14	12	14	12	14	12	13
13	17	13	17	13	15	13	15	13	15	13	15	13	14	13	15	13	15	13	15	13	15	13	14
14	18	14	18	14	16	14	16	14	16	14	16	14	15	14	16	14	16	14	16	14	16	14	15
15	19	15	19	15	17	15	17	15	17	15	17	15	16	15	17	15	17	15	17	15	17	15	16
16	20	16	20	16	18	16	18	16	18	16	18	16	17	16	18	16	18	16	18	16	18	16	17
17	21	17	21	17	19	17	19	17	19	17	19	17	18	17	19	17	19	17	19	17	19	17	18
18	22	18	22	18	20	18	20	18	20	18	20	18	19	18	20	18	20	18	20	18	20	18	19
19	23	19	23	19	21	19	21	19	21	19	21	19	20	19	21	19	21	19	21	19	21	19	20
20	24	20	24	20	22	20	22	20	22	20	22	20	21	20	22	20	22	20	22	20	22	20	21
21	25	21	25	21	23	21	23	21	23	21	23	21	22	21	23	21	23	21	23	21	23	21	22
22	26	22	26	22	24	22	24	22	24	22	24	22	23	22	24	22	24	22	24	22	24	22	23
23	27	23	27	23	25	23	25	23	25	23	25	23	24	23	25	23	25	23	25	23	25	23	24
24	28	24	28	24	26	24	26	24	26	24	26	24	25	24	26	24	26	24	26	24	26	24	25
25	29	25	29	25	27	25	27	25	27	25	27	25	26	25	27	25	27	25	27	25	27	25	26
26	30	26	30	26	28	26	28	26	28	26	28	26	27	26	28	26	28	26	28	26	28	26	27
27	31	27	May 1	27	29	27	29	27	29	27	29	27	28	27	29	27	29	27	29	27	29	27	28
28	Apl. 1	28	2	28	30	28	30	28	30	28	30	28	29	28	30	28	30	28	30	28	30	28	Mar 1
29	2	29	3	29	31	29	July 1	29	31	29	31	29	30	29	31	29	31	29	31	29	31	29	2
30	3	—	—	30	June 1	30	2	30	Aug 1	30	Sept 1	30	Oct 1	30	Nov 1	30	Dec 2	30	Jan 1	30	Feb 1	30	3
31	4	—	—	31	2	—	—	31	2	31	—	31	2	31	2	31	—	31	2	—	—	31	4

Cairn Terrier about to whelp. Note the excellent whelping box with 'let down' solid section at front to keep puppies in and the draught out, the mesh upper section. This box also has a hinged lid.

and lowered as required.

As the amount of power used by these lamps is about 250 watts, it is quite a cheap method of heating. However, do not make the mistake of using a heating lamp which gives a white heat, as the light will be far too bright.

A day or two prior to the date of whelping the hair on the abdomen and hindquarters of a long-coated bitch should be cut back. This will facilitate attending to her during parturition. At the same time the nipples and underparts should be bathed with warm water containing a little non-carbolic disinfectant. This will remove both dirt and any eggs of parasitic worms that may have been picked up from the ground.

Some thought should also be given to the equipment which may be required when whelping begins. Such things as towels, cotton wool, squares of flannel or similar soft material, a pair of surgical scissors, glucose, a small quantity of brandy, Vaseline or liquid paraffin, and a good 'safe' disinfectant like Dettol, should be in readiness in case of need. Though it is unwise to anticipate trouble, it is as well to be prepared for an emergency and to notify a veterinary surgeon of the date the bitch is due. Let him see her a day or two before and arrange for him to be on call should skilled assistance be required in a hurry.

CHAPTER 9

WHELPING

The normal period of gestation in a bitch is sixty-three days from the time of fertilisation, and this is not necessarily the time of mating. If a bitch has been mated a day or so too early, the eggs may not have been fertilised until a day or two after the mating, and consequently when the expected date for whelping arrives, the owner can become anxious without good cause.

Healthy litters can be born five days early, or two days late, but anything outside this period can mean trouble. A premature litter which survives the first twenty-four hours has a fair chance of survival if sufficient time and care is spent on it. A premature litter is one born six or more days early. A bitch should not be allowed to go beyond the sixty-sixth day without veterinary advice being sought. If there is any sign of a discharge from the vagina, or the bitch being in any way distressed, professional help should be called immediately. It is not always easy to know how near a bitch is to whelping by her behaviour, as she may be restless, tear at her bedding to make a 'nest', or hide under things and so on, for several days before the onset of labour. The surest sign is a drop in temperature from the normal 101·5° to about 98° or even lower in some cases. In some bitches, there is a very sharp fall in temperature, whilst others take much longer. When this drop starts, labour is usually about to start within the next 24 hours.

Parturition may occur at any time but is most usual at night or in the early morning hours. If a bitch seems restless, or ill at ease, when put to bed at night, she should be visited two or three times during the hours of darkness in case labour starts and she needs assistance. Some bitches, especially those expecting first litters, become very excited and agitated, roaming from room to room if in the house, or dashing round their kennels if outdoors, scratching in corners and tearing up their beds, two or three days before they actually whelp. Others are quiet and restrained up to the last moment.

When labour starts a bitch generally goes to her box or bed. She may stretch out at full length, begin to pant or shiver, then get up, turn round and lie down again, as though unable to get comfortable. As the pains increase she may whine, her head towards her hindquarters, snap at her flanks, then sit down with her quarters pressed against the side of the box. Examination will show the vulva is swollen and that there is a thick mucous discharge. If labour pains are sustained, a puppy may be born within half an hour or so, but if the pains pass, or are weak and intermittent, it may be several hours before the first whelp appears.

Labour may precede birth by anything from a few minutes to three hours. The interval is usually longer in a bitch having her first litter than in a matron, and shorter in a young bitch than in an old one, if both are whelping for the first time. If labour continues fruitlessly for longer than three hours a veterinary surgeon should be called, as there may be a serious complication, such as a very awkwardly placed puppy, which must be dealt with before parturition can proceed. Left to her own devices in such circumstances a bitch may exhaust herself by repeated straining and the final result be the death of all the puppies and, possibly, of the bitch herself.

When the time for birth arrives a puppy must be delivered quickly if it is to live. Should circumstances arise to delay its emergence into the outside world, remedial measures must be taken speedily. The presence of a dead puppy is indicated by a thick greenish discharge which soon becomes offensive and turns reddish brown. This is an urgent danger signal. Veterinary help must be obtained at once for, unless the dead puppy is removed without delay, there will be little chance of saving the mother.

The uterine contractions that precede birth are, in the main, automatic or reflex, but they can be affected by emotional or mental stress. In a highly strung bitch having her first litter, labour may be inhibited by a nervous, hysterical condition. The owner of a bitch of that kind should be in attendance from the beginning of labour until all the puppies have been born and the dam is settled comfortably with her family. The aim must be to give her a feeling of confidence and security. As with a frightened child, the sound of a familiar voice making soothing and encouraging noises will often do more than anything else to overcome fear and prevent panic. On the other hand, a bitch that has been much fussed and petted may be better if left alone when parturition is imminent. The presence of human companions may cause her to desire and expect lavish demonstrations of affection and while she is in that mental state labour may be protracted or inhibited. If left she will probably whelp normally but while anyone is there to hold her hand she will do nothing to help herself. But, though most healthy bitches may be expected to cope with matters satisfactorily without interference, an unobtrusive watch should be maintained so that, should assistance of any kind be needed, it may be immediately forthcoming. The majority of difficulties that crop up during whelping may be quickly and easily dealt with by a watchful observer, but if help is not at the right moment a valuable puppy, or perhaps a whole litter, may be lost.

Parturition may be delayed through the uterine contractions being too weak or infrequent to start things moving. Uterine inertia may occur in bitches of any age or in any breed but is more common in untried bitches than in those which have been bred from previously, and in some breeds more than in others. Bitches that are fat or in soft condition are especially prone to the trouble. Injections of a uterine stimulant, like pituitrin, are usually effective in hastening delivery.

In a bitch the uterus consists of a basal portion which is divided into two extensions called the uterine horns. Under normal conditions the uterine contractions are sufficiently strong to cause the young whelp, enclosed in its fluid-filled envelope, to move down from its position in one of the horns to the body of the womb, whence it is expelled into the vagina, from which it passes through the external aperture of the vagina. As a rule the sac in which it is enclosed bursts as the puppy is born. Normally the youngster emerges head first, with the forelegs stretched out in front of the body. The foetal membranes may be still attached to, and come away with, the puppy, or the umbibed cord may be severed as birth occurs and the afterbirth remain behind, to be subsequently expelled by a strong contraction of the uterus and vagina. When rupture of the sac is not followed by the birth of the puppy the bitch should be examined. If the whelp can be seen or felt, delivery may generally be achieved by careful manual manipulation. The puppy should be grasped behind the head and pulled steadily downwards as the bitch strains. If there is some difficulty in getting a hold on the whelp with the bare hands, a piece of flannel of suitable size will make it easier to grasp the slippery surface.

A puppy which emerges still ensheathed in its envelope must be released at once. The dam will usually attend to this, but should she fail to do so the sac must be opened above the nostrils and gently worked off the body. The cord should be held tightly between thumb and forefinger, about an inch from the body, ligatured with silk and cut with surgical scissors. Bitches of very short-faced breeds are often incapable of releasing their puppies and an attendant should always be present to give whatever assistance may be required. Some bitches are very rough with their new born young. When severing the cord they may pull part of the intestine out of position, causing umbilical hernia, or injure a puppy about the head and body as the membranes are removed. Where there is a risk of youngsters suffering in this way they should be taken from the dam as they are born and released by hand. Having severed the cord and released a whelp the bitch may devour the foetal envelope. This is quite natural and in no way deleterious. Immediately a puppy is born the dam should lick it vigorously, thereby stimulating circulation and inducing it to breathe. If, for some reason, she is unable or unwilling to attend to it, the puppy should be rubbed with a piece of soft flannel or cotton wool, special care being taken to clear the nostrils.

If it does not occur naturally, breathing should be started by opening the mouth, depressing the tongue and blowing several times down the throat. Alternatively the forelegs may be moved backward and forwards, or the ribs tapped sharply with a cold, wet cloth. A drop of brandy on the tongue will often bring a response even from a seemingly lifeless puppy.

In some cases, as when there is a very large or badly placed puppy, natural birth may be impossible and recourse must be had to a caesarian section, in which the uterus is opened and the young whelp extracted. The operation is safe and effective, and does not exhaust a bitch anything like as much as does long, fruitless labour, provided it is performed in good time—that is, while the bitch is strong and fresh. Unfortunately matters are often left until the mother has become weak and exhausted, so that even if the operation is successful recovery is slow and may necessitate sacrificing part of the litter. If all goes well a caesarian section should not prejudicially affect a bitch. At her next whelping parturition may be normal and easy.

After the birth of the first puppy others may be expected to arrive at intervals of from fifteen minutes to two hours. With a litter of moderate size—up to six puppies—whelping may be completed within three hours, but where the litter is larger it may take much longer; labour pains abating for some time after five or six whelps have been born. If she is whelping normally a bitch is best left undisturbed until all her puppies have arrived, but should there be difficulty or delays and she seems distressed or shows signs of exhaustion, she should be given a drink of milk and glucose into which a little brandy has been stirred.

If, after whelping seems to have finished, the bitch is restless or uneasy, the presence of one or more unborn puppies may be suspected and unless prompt action is taken she may become feverish and refuse to take interest in the young ones already born. A veterinary surgeon should be called in at once, so that appropriate measures may be taken to induce a resumption of parturition.

Some breeders consider it advisable to take the puppies from the bitch as they are born, and have been cleaned; transferring them to a warm, flannel-lined box or basket.The object is to avoid the risk of the dam pushing them aside or injuring them during the delivery of the later born whelps. This is unnecessary unless the dam is clumsy or nervous. As a rule a bitch is very carcful and may be worried if her whelps are taken from her. If the young are removed the greatest care must be taken to ensure that they are kept very warm until they are returned to the nest.

When all the litter has arrived the bitch should be taken out for a few minutes and given an opportunity of emptying her bladder and bowels. In her absence the floor covering of the whelping box should be renewed and everything cleaned up. The puppies should be handled very gently and as little as possible. They may be checked for sex and any that are deformed taken away and destroyed. This must, of course, be done out of sight and hearing of the mother.

The novice breeder should not be tempted to discard puppies which soon after birth show characteristics not typical of adults of the breed. For the first few days all puppies appear to be smooth, whatever kind of coat their parents wear, and all have drop ears. The nose and lips, especially in white or particoloured puppies, are often wholly or partially pink. Normally these parts will darken gradually with age and by the sixth or seventh week will probably be black. Coat colour, too, may be deceptive. Generally the colour is darker than it will be in the adult. This applies to most breeds but is especially marked in Bedlington Terriers, Kerry Blues, Airedales, Dandy Dinmonts, Yorkshires and in Blue and Silver Poodles, in which the coat is at first almost or quite black. By contrast, Dalmation puppies are born white, the spots beginning to appear when they are two or three weeks old. Small markings on chest, toes and muzzle in babies of varieties in which solid colour is desired need cause no anxiety, as they are likely to disappear in a few weeks. There is a tendency for white markings of all kinds to decrease rather than to increase in size as a puppy grows. Remember, too, that size at birth is not a reliable guide to the size which a puppy will eventually reach. The smallest member of a litter may grow into the biggest adult, and the largest may in a few weeks be outgrown by its smaller brothers and sisters.

CHAPTER 10

THE NURSING MOTHER

ON THE COMPLETION of whelping the bitch should be made comfortable and offered a drink of warm milk-food, such as egg, milk and glucose. If she refuses it no effort should be made to force it on her. What she now needs is rest and to be left quietly with her new family. Her temperature may be somewhat above normal for a time, but as long as it does not mount above one hundred and three degrees there is no need to worry. Should it go above that level however, or remain well above normal for more than a few days, a veterinary surgeon should be asked to examine her. High temperature with fits of shivering and lack of appetite may be symptomatic of serious trouble. Part of an afterbirth, or even a dead puppy, may remain in the uterus, and delay in removing it may cause septicaemia or metritis (inflammation of the womb).

For a week or so there will be some discharge from the vagina but this should gradually decrease. If it continues much longer than a week or becomes copious with rising temperature, a veterinary surgeon should be consulted. For a day or two the bowels will be loose, the motions being black and liquid. This is normal but the condition should continue only for a few days. If it goes on longer, or if there is a tendency towards constipation, castor oil or liquid paraffin should be given.

A newly whelped bitch should be kept on a light, easily digested diet. For a couple of days she should have only liquid foods, such as egg and milk (one yolk to a pint of milk), one of the proprictary milk preparations or thin gruel. On the third day wholemeal rusks soaked in milk or broth, with tripe or fish, may be added. This menu should be continued for the next three days. Such a diet will provide all the nourishment necessary, help to keep the temperature from rising and rest the digestive organs.

Overloading the stomach before it has recovered its tone is likely to give rise to digestive upsets which may make a bitch so uncomfortable that she becomes unwilling, or unable, satisfactorily to look after her puppies.

Too generous a diet at this time will also encourage premature stimulation of the milk flow before the whelps are vigorous enough to cope with it. This may result in the formation of breast abcesses, or make the teats so swollen and hard that the puppies are unable to feed. If a light diet as recommended is continued for seven days after parturition, milk will be produced in quantities sufficient to satisfy the requirements of the young family without burdening the dam with an embarrassing surplus. At the end of a week the mother's diet may be increased and from then until the puppies are weaned should be generous and rich in protein and vitamins. Raw lean meat, eggs, strong broth, milk, wholemeal rusks or biscuit meal, plus a daily dose of fish-liver oil, calcium and yeast tablets, or some other source of Vitamin B, should keep a bitch in glowing health and enable her to provide adequately for her growing babies.

At first the proud mother will probably be unwilling to leave her litter even for short periods. She must, however, be taken out for five minutes or so at least four times a day to empty her bladder and bowels. From the third day the periods should be increased to fifteen minutes and by the end of the week she should be having regular walks or spells of free exercise and be encouraged to spend some time away from her family in the open air. Plenty of exercise is necessary to stimulate lactation.

Most bitches soon settle down eagerly to the routine of motherhood, suckling and caring for their puppies by instinct. Occasionally, however, a young bitch may be so over-excited or distracted after the ordeal of whelping that for a time she refuses to take any interest in her offspring. She may even resent any efforts made by the questing youngsters to attach themselves to her teats. A bitch of this kind should be spoken to quietly, made much of and, if necessary, given a mild sedative. When she is quiet the puppies may be put to her. If a whelp fails to grasp a teat its mouth should be opened, a nipple inserted and a little milk squeezed out by gentle pressure. This will usually start it sucking. Sometimes it may be necessary to hold the bitch while the puppies feed. After her first nervousness has been overcome the mother may accept the importunities of her family and thenceforth give no trouble. Where there is persistent refusal to nurse, the puppies should be allowed to feed for from ten to twenty minutes while the dam is forcibly controlled. It may be necessary to repeat this for a day or two, after which the bitch, providing she is well and normal in temperament, will probably prove a satisfactory mother.

Later, as the puppies grow, refusal to suckle may be due to excess of milk causing the breasts to be hard, inflamed and painful. Relief may be given by bathing the glands with hot water every half hour and massaging with warm camphorated oil. Some milk should be drawn off as soon as the breasts are soft enough to be handled without giving pain to the bitch, and when it is flowing freely the puppies may be put to suck. Unless speedy relief is given the bitch may become feverish and it will be found that abscesses have formed. Hot fomentations should be applied at once and continued until each abscess comes to a head, when it may be lanced, if it does not burst to discharge its contents. As soon as this occurs pain will subside, the temperature drop to normal and the puppies may be returned, to the dam. An inverted or indrawn nipple may be brought out by massaging it between the forefinger and thumb, or by placing the rim of a warmed bottle of suitable size over the affected teat. As the bottle cools the nipple will be drawn out.

A bitch with a small litter, after nursing well for a time, may suddenly become restless and irritable. Examination will probably show that some of the teats have been neglected and are hard and inflamed. They must be attended to quickly or the pain may cause the bitch to refuse to have the puppies near her, so that they have to be prematurely weaned and reared by hand. The breasts should be treated as suggested above and when relief has been given care taken to see that all the teats are sucked; the puppies being changed about at each feed instead of being left to feed from only a few of the nipples.

Sore and cracked nipples are apt to occur after a bitch has nursed a litter for a fortnight or so. The condition is usually caused by the erupting teeth and sharp claws of the rapidly growing puppies. The affected parts should be bathed, dried carefully and dusted with boric powder. It may be necessary to remove the puppies for a few days to enable the abrasions to heal. The claws of young puppies grow quickly and soon become needle sharp. A nursing bitch often suffers much from punctures and scratches inflicted on her tender breasts by the clawing of her whelps. Puppies' claws should be kept short and blunt by being clipped once or twice prior to weaning. Continual crying by puppies with refusal to suck for more than a few minutes at a time and stomachs which seem to be only partly filled after feeding, indicates that the mother's milk is either deficient in quantity or is too acid. Acidity may be remedied by mixing bicarbonate of soda—a heaped teaspoonful to a pint—to all liquids offered to the bitch, or by giving her daily doses of milk of magnesia.

A bitch usually keeps her whelps scrupulously clean by attending to their toilet after each feed and at other times as necessary. Some mothers, however, seem to be lacking in the instinct to carry out this duty so that their youngsters look scruffy, soiled and dull-coated. When a bitch is negligent in this way her puppies should be cleaned by hand after each meal. All dried milk and other detritus should be carefully removed with a pad of cotton wool soaked in warm water. If crusts have formed they should be softened with a little Vaseline before being dealt with. The abdomen and anus must be cleaned and gently massaged. This will encourage regular bowel action. Puppies usually open their eyes between the tenth and the fourteenth day. Until they are fully open and the youngsters are crawling about, the nest should be kept in semi-darkness. If placed in too strong a light the eyes may remain closed for two or three days longer than in dimmer surroundings. If opened earlier the sight may be impaired. Normally the eyes are kept clean by the dam's tongue, but if there is any discharge it should be removed by swabbing with warm boric lotion and the edges of the lids may be lightly smeared with golden eye ointment.

In breeds in which the tail is shortened or docked this should be done when the puppies are from three to five days old. Dew claws, if present, may be removed at the same time.

Cairn Terrier Bitch belonging to Mrs. Harding 'Brucairn' Cairns, suckling four

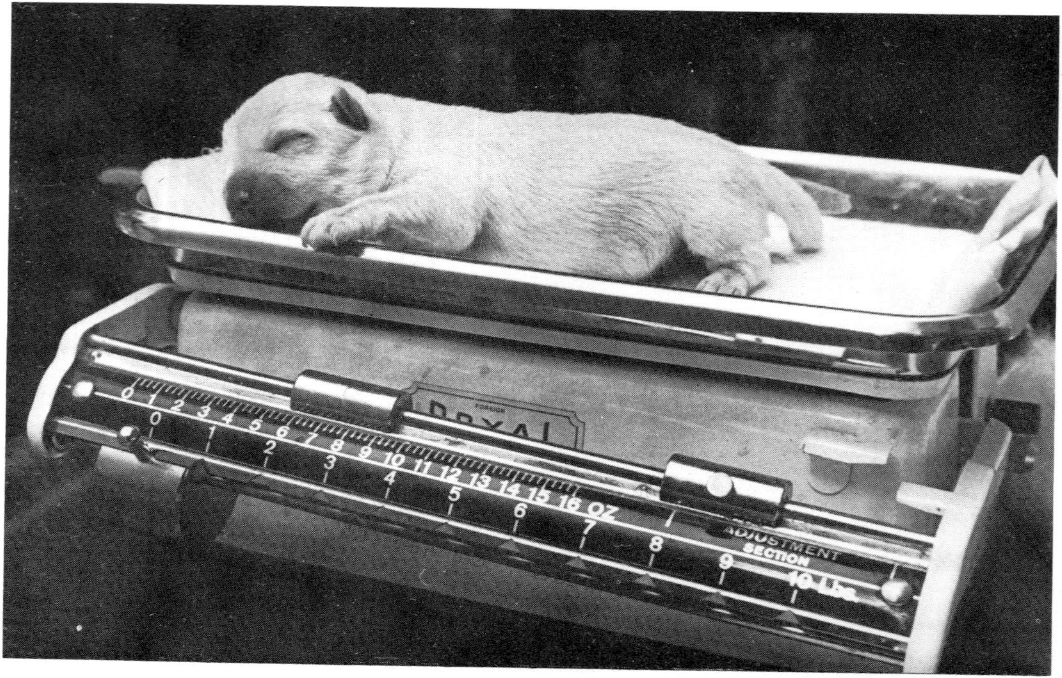

A new born whelp being 'weighed-in'

CHAPTER 11

THE CARE OF YOUNG PUPPIES

FOR ABOUT a week after birth puppies make very few demands on their dam as regards the provision of food. In these early days their principal need is warmth. A very young puppy has very little natural heat and if it is pushed aside by its dam, or crowded out by its litter mates, it may become chilled and torpid unless precautions are taken to keep the whole nest really warm. If the kennel or whelping box can be maintained at a minimum temperature of seventy-five degrees and the bitch is attentive, artificial heating is not necessary, but the use of hot-water bottles, well covered and placed under the bedding, is a great help in keeping the young family comfortable. If whelping takes place in an outdoor kennel some form of heating is almost essential, except during the warmest days of summer. Should a puppy be separated from the others, or be neglected by its dam, it should be put into a softly lined box or basket and kept near a source of heat until it is thoroughly warm and lively before being returned to the nest.

A whelp which was not quite as strong as its companions at birth may, during the next few days, be found to be losing ground. It may fail to suck and receive little attention from its mother. When handled its stomach will probably feel almost empty, its body be limp and its coat rough. If isolated and kept very warm in an airing cupboard, on a shelf above the oven or even in an oven, and given hourly doses of glucose and water at blood heat from a small pipette or dropper, there is a good chance that it will recover. When put back with the rest of the litter, it may prove to be strong enough to hold its own.

If their dam's milk is plentiful and of good quality the puppies should thrive without any set-backs. There are, however, a few slight disorders that may affect them but which may be easily dealt with if noticed in time. Milk that is somewhat acid, though not sufficiently so to cause the youngster to refuse to feed, may give rise to slight stomach upsets and a characteristic rash. The coat looks dull or staring and the hair may fall out in patches, leaving flaky sores or scabs. The remedy is to add bicarbonate of soda to the bitch's food. See that she has ample exercise. Bathe the patches or sores on the puppies with a weak solution of Dettol or T.C.P., and after drying dress with olive oil or boric ointment. A slight rash under the chin and on the abdomen, which may be accompanied by irritation, may be due to overheating of the blood or to a small digestive trouble. It usually disappears in a few days if dressed with castor oil and zinc ointment. Diluted T.C.P. will quickly allay the irritation.

Very young puppies sometimes suffer from prolapsus of the anus. This is caused by straining in efforts to pass the faeces, resulting in a small portion of the lower bowel being forced out. The protruding part must be pressed back into place with a small swab of cotton wool lubricated with glycerine or Vaseline. The puppy must be watched and should the protuberance reappear it must be pressed back again. Olive oil or liquid paraffin should be given to keep the motions loose. If prolapsus persists the puppy should be taken from the nest, kept warm in a well-lined box or basket and returned to its dam at intervals to feed. Should there be no improvement after twenty-four hours veterinary advice should be obtained, as a minor operation may be necessary.

A whelp which does not make satisfactory progress during the first week and seems to be losing rather than gaining weight on the small quantity of milk it takes from its dam, may be given one or two small feeds of raw meat daily, even at this tender age. The meat must be very finely scraped and pressed through a sieve before being fed from a spoon. If a puppy looks dehydrated, with dry skin and lolling head, glucose and water should be given every hour. The supplementary feeding of meat juice with frequent drinks of glucose may be practised with a whole litter when the dam's milk is insufficient to satisfy the puppies. This is preferable to hand-feeding with milk, as it is less likely to discourage feeding from the mother and will give quicker results.

Normally, however, all should go well, with the dam supplying all the nutriment needed by the growing babies, until the end of the third week. At that age the first teeth will probably have pierced the gums and the puppies may have their first taste of solid food. This is given in the form of finely scraped raw, lean meat.

There will be no difficulty in getting the youngsters to take this; on the contrary, the tendency is for too much to be given at a time. For puppies of medium-sized breeds as much as will roll into a ball the size of a marble is ample.

One feed each day is sufficient for a week or ten days, after which two may be given. Because the raw meat is taken so eagerly a breeder may be tempted to increase the ration too quickly. This will cause digestive disorders and the puppies may lose their appetite for milk; showing little or no desire to suck and will take less liquid nourishment than is required to keep them fit and comfortable. When handled, their abdomens may feel hard and congested, their coats look dull and their motions be irregular or constipated. The remedy is to reduce the meat feeds, or to cut them out altogether until matters right themselves and the youngsters are again feeding well and eagerly from their dam. If the amount of meat given is reasonably restricted and increased very gradually, so as to keep pace with body growth, no such trouble will occur.

By the fourth week supplementary milk foods may be introduced with advantage. Egg and milk (one egg beaten up in a pint of warm milk) or one of the proprietary products prepared for nursery or kennel use, are recommended. If available, goat's milk is excellent. The food should be given at blood heat. At first very little is required. Some puppies are slower than others to learn to lap but with a little patience any youngster may be taught to take liquid from a spoon or saucer in three days. Start with one small meal a day and gradually increase until, when six weeks old, the puppies are receiving five meals daily. This number should be maintained until the tenth week, when one feed may be dropped (usually a milk feed).

From the sixth week Farex, crumbled or broken wholemeal rusks or fine biscuit meal may be added to one of the milk feeds, or given with broth or gravy from which the fat has been removed, or mixed with beaten raw eggs. If weaning is made a gradual process by introducing supplementary feeds from three weeks onwards, as suggested, the change over from mother's milk to other food and a more varied diet may be effected without any trouble and without causing distress to either the mother or her puppies. By following this method weaning occurs naturally and by the end of the fifth week the youngsters will be independent of their dam.

A puppy which tends to lose weight after being weaned may usually be put right by a short course of Parrish's Chemical Food or Radio Malt. The latter is a fine conditioner for a poor doer and will improve an indifferent appetite. The amount of food offered will, of course, vary with the size of the puppies and their individual needs, but no more should be given at a meal than is eagerly eaten without distending the stomach unduly. A well-fed puppy should look plump and solid, but overloading the digestive organs with bulky, starchy food must be avoided. If the body becomes too fat, it may be too heavy for the immature limbs to support and result in faulty shoulders, pasterns and quarters with, possibly, loose elbows and bowed fore legs.

At six weeks old a suitable diet may be based on the following.

FIRST MEAL: Egg and milk, or other milk food, with Farex, crumbled wholemeal rusks, or fine biscuit meal.
SECOND MEAL: Minced or scraped raw, lean meat, cooked liver, fish or tripe, with stale wholemeal bread. The whole to be moistened with good stock or gravy.
THIRD MEAL: Milk food thickened with Farex, Beemax, oatmeal or other cereal.
FOURTH MEAL: Raw meat or egg mixed with wholemeal crumbs or soaked, kibbled rusks.
FIFTH MEAL: A drink of milk food.

At this age meat or its equivalent in protein value should account for one-third to one-half the weight of all food given. From the fifth week until it is fully grown each puppy should have a daily dose of fish-liver oil and calcium. If wholemeal rusks or meals are used there should be no need to provide additional vitamin B, but yeast tablets are very useful for keeping skin and coat in good condition and warding off teething troubles.

As the puppies grow their food should include less liquid. The meat may be cut into small pieces instead of being minced, and later given in lumps. The cereal ingredients may be fed either moist or dry. Sloppy food of any kind should be avoided as soon as more solid fare can be dealt with satisfactorily.

There is no specific time when a puppy should be transferred to a normal adult diet, this depends on the breed and the general development of the individual. Usually a puppy will let you know when it is ready to start cutting out a meal by just refusing to have anything to do with it. Generally, the afternoon milk feed is the first to be discarded, and then one of the two meat meals. A puppy that hasn't experienced hunger will tell you when enough is enough.

Sunshine and fresh air are as essential to robust health as are suitable food and regular meal times. No effort should be spared to give puppies access to these vitalising influences from the time they are firmly on their legs. Freedom to play in the open with a warm, dry bed to go to when tired are among the requisites for successful puppy rearing.

Young puppies should sleep at frequent intervals. Rest after a meal is especially beneficial. If a romp precedes a meal the fully-fed youngsters will be ready to retire to their sleeping quarters for a period, but if kept shut up in a small kennel throughout the day they will become bored and fretful and soon lose both appetite and condition. Long continued close confinement may make puppies nervous, lethargic and mentally dull and is a common cause of unsoundness in later life.

Six week old Alsatian puppies bred by Anne MacDonald "Hanovarian" Alsatians and Keeshonds. Note the excellent bone. The ears on alsatian puppies do not rise for some time but are usually erect by the age of four months.

Weimaramer puppy, bred by Mrs. Veasey

Yellow Labrador puppy, bred by Miss Casson

CHAPTER 12

FOSTERING AND HAND-REARING PUPPIES

IT SOMETIMES happens that a bitch which has had a very prolonged or difficult whelping refuses to have anything to do with her newly-born family and the owner is faced by the problem of deciding how the litter shall be reared. There are two alternatives. The puppies may be handed over to a foster mother or efforts may be made to rear them by hand. If a satisfactory foster can be procured there is little more to worry about. There is not likely to be much trouble in getting her to adopt her charges. The foster may be of any breed, but she should be of about the same size as the natural mother and she should have whelped not more than two or three days previously—the younger the puppies are the better. The two litters should be placed together in a small box so that they come in to close contact with one another. In this way the babies that are to be given to the foster will acquire the scent of her own whelps.

When the bitch is settled in her bed the puppies to be adopted should be introduced one by one quietly and without fuss. If possible the change over should be made at night or in semi-darkness. Usually the foster will accept the changelings without trouble, but she should be watched until she has snuggled them against her and started to lick them. Thereafter all should go smoothly. For small breeds a cat often makes an excellent foster if a bitch cannot be procured. She is quiet, gentle and very devoted to her charges. A small cat will rear three or four puppies with ease, even when they are as large and lusty as young alsatians. This is admirably illustrated on Plate 9. In the case depicted, the dam of the puppies, after a very bad whelping and subsequent complications, had to be taken from her litter. Four of the surviving whelps were fostered by the cat, together with her own kitten. Mrs Margaret Barron the owner, writes: 'The cat fed and washed the puppies and gave them warmth at night. They were quickly trained to be clean in the nest by the cat, who cried as soon as there was any mess in the basket. At three weeks old the dog puppy was crying to be lifted out of the basket to perform natural functions. At a fortnight old the cat took lumps of half chewed raw meat from her own dish and tucked them under the puppies' heads so that they could suck them when they awoke instead of screaming for her to feed them. All the puppies thrived and reached full maturity without ever looking back.'

Unfortunately, a newly whelped bitch or an accommodating cat is not usually available when needed as a foster, and hand-rearing becomes necessary. This is not particularly difficult but it calls for much patience and a good deal of time. Apart from that, natural nursing has so many advantages that every possible endeavour should be made to encourage it even when it seems almost hopeless. Even the most obstinate mother may sometimes be persuaded to allow her young ones to feed from her for the first few days, even if only at intervals, if she is treated with kindness allied to firmness and, if absolutely necessary, placed under some slight restraint. Quite often a bitch which is at first stubbornly disinclined to suckle her puppies or look after them in any way, loses her antipathy after a few days when, under the stimulus of sucking, her milk flow is satisfactorily established. Even if an inadequate milk supply necessitates supplementary feeding and early weaning, puppies which have had short or spasmodic periods of natural feeding are usually stronger, more resistant to disease and parasites, and generally easier to rear than those which have to be artificially fed from birth.

If, however, the mother dies, succumbs to serious illness or proves adamant in her refusal to nurse them, the puppies must be hand-reared. When this befalls, here is the procedure. For the first week the babies must be fed every two hours through the day and night and the box in which they are kept must be maintained at a minimum temperature of seventy-five degrees. The floor should be well-covered with blankets, under which one or more hot water-bottles may be slipped. Warmth, and complete protection from draughts and damp, is of supreme importance.

The most suitable food is one of the dried milk preparations manufactured for puppies or for children, full-cream goat's milk to which a little glucose or honey may be added, or the egg and milk mixture already referred to, plus three tablespoonfuls of extra cream. A drop or two of halibut liver oil should be mixed with the first and last feeds. From the first, the food given should be of thick, creamy consistency. If the whelps are to thrive their food must approximate closely to bitch's milk, which is very rich in proteins and fat as compared with that of the cow, as the following table shows:

PERCENTAGE COMPOSITION OF MILK

Species	*Water*	*Fat*	*Sugar*	*Protein*
Dog	75.44	9.57	3.09	11.15
Goat	82.34	7.57	4.96	4.22
Cow	87.32	3.75	4.75	3.40
Man	88.50	3.30	6.80	1.30

From this it will be understood why goat's milk is generally recommended for puppies in preference to cow's milk. But, though richer than cow's milk, the richest sample of goat's milk is very much poorer in protein than that of the average bitch. For human babies cow and goat milk is often diluted to reduce the fat and protein content to the level of mother's milk, but for young puppies both need to be enriched. The powdered milk products prepared for babies are often used for puppy rearing. These preparations are made to formulae based on the needs of human babies and when mixed with water in the proportions advised on the tin or package the fluid closely resembles human milk in chemical composition. When used for puppies only about a half the volume of water recommended for baby feeding should be added to the powder.

The easiest method of feeding is by means of a small pipette or dropper. While being fed the puppy should be held in such a way that the liquid is placed drop by drop on to the back of the tongue. This is a slow, tedious job but any attempt to hurry matters will cause digestive troubles. Each meal should take at least ten minutes. As the whelps grow a small feeding bottle may be used, special care being taken that the milk does not flow too freely. Hand-fed puppies usually learn to lap from a spoon at a very early age, so that bottles may not be required. They are, however, very useful when there are several puppies to be cared for.

All food must be given in small quantities, the actual amount required depending on the breed concerned. The stomach of a young puppy is small—in the small breeds not much larger than a pigeon's egg—and is soon filled. If during the first two weeks a puppy seems backward and lacking in vitality, a fragment of Brand's Essence, or a few drops of the juice pressed from a piece of raw steak, given once daily, often effects a marked improvement.

At the end of the first week a feed every three hours will suffice and after a further fortnight the interval between meals may be increased to four hours.

After each feed, each puppy must be cleaned with cotton wool moistened with a weak solution of a mild disinfectant. Bowel action must be induced by gently massaging the abdomen and rectum with a flannel dipped in warm water, in imitation of the action of the dam, who licks her whelps vigorously on those parts after they have fed. Should any sign of constipation appear a few drops of olive oil or liquid paraffin on the back of the tongue twice daily should soon put matters right. Unless regular defecation is maintained acute gastric or bowel disorders are likely to develop which may persist and gravely jeopardise the youngster's chances of survival.

CHAPTER 13

BREEDING IN WINTER

IT WAS AT one time customary for older breeders to caution a novice with the words 'Never mate a bitch before the shortest day or after the longest'. There is certainly much to be said for this view, but circumstances may arise which make an owner of a bitch particularly eager to have a litter from her during the winter months. A keen exhibitor may wish to have some young stock ready for competition in the puppy classes at the summer and autumn shows, or the bitch from which it is intended to breed may come in season only once in twelve months or so, so that, if she is to be mated at all, there is not much choice about when she shall be sent to a stud dog. There is no reason why the winter breeding should be rigorously eschewed, but if a bitch is to whelp and rear a litter successfully during the coldest months she must be given extra care and attention.

As has been emphasised in a former chapter, a pregnant bitch must be kept in hard, muscular condition. This is possible only if she has adequate outdoor exercise right up to the time when her growing girth and increasing weight make it unwise and unsafe to allow her to take long walks or to indulge in strenuous romps or gallops.

But in winter it is usually much more difficult to provide regular daily exercise than in spring and summer. Weather conditions are more likely to render outdoor excursions uncomforable for the owner, if not for the bitch, and there is the probability that road and field work will be restricted. If the bitch comes home wet or muddy from a walk special care must be taken to see that she is dried and cleaned thoroughly before going to her kennel or box.

Even while confined to a kennel-run the bitch will require closer supervision than in summer. As she becomes heavier she will tend to sit about in the open instead of keeping on the move, and in the damp or wet days to be expected at this season there is a grave risk of her contracting a chill which, besides being serious in itself, may, by lowering her resistance, be the forerunner of other infections. Rather than keeping a pregnant bitch confined during a spell of rainy or snowy weather, it is preferable to let her take a reasonable amount of exercise out of doors.

See that she is kept moving briskly and is well rubbed down on her return. This applies to normally hardy breeds. A toy bitch may be given all the exercise she requires to keep her fit indoors during inclement weather.

Special consideration must also be given to the provision of whelping accommodation. It must be warm, absolutely dry and draught-proof. From the time whelping is imminent some kind of artificial heating must be provided, so that a temperature of seventy-five degrees may be assured. More puppies are lost in the first two weeks of their lives from cold than from any other cause, and the mortality is a good deal higher in winter-bred litters than in those born in spring and summer.

It should be clearly understood that the first week or two after birth is the most critical in a puppy's life. It has very little natural warmth and is almost wholly dependent for survival on the temperature of its surroundings. In winter, even in a warm room or heated kennel, additional sources of heat in the nest itself are advisable. Perhaps the easiest way to provide this is by means of hot-water bottles or bags. They should be well-covered with flannel or blanketing to obviate any risk of the puppies being injured by coming in contact with the hot surface. If this precaution is observed the bottles may be placed in the nest after being fitted with near-boiling water, and will remain hot for a surprisingly long time, diffusing a gentle, moist heat which is beneficial and comforting to both bitch and puppies. The more modern infra-red lamps are available at very reasonable prices and eliminate the need for the periodic changing of bottles. Care must be taken, however, to see that a lamp is not placed too low over the nest, otherwise the dry heat may cause skin trouble, and be prejudicial to general health.

Each time the dam is taken out for exercise she must be thoroughly dried and her underparts sponged over before she is allowed to go back to her litter. She must on no account be left out too long without supervision as, if she sits down or lies on wet ground, or sits about in chilly wind, metritis or inflammation of the womb (*see* page 55) may ensue. When the puppies are strong on their legs they will need more room than is available to them in the confines of the nest and will probably have to be moved to more commodious quarters. Here, too, the temperature must be controlled, so that it does not drop below sixty-five degrees, and all draughts must be excluded.

At three weeks, supplementary meals of finely scraped raw meat and milk food may be started, but winter-born puppies should be left with their dam as long as she will tolerate them. The presence of their mother at intervals through the day and all through the night will help to keep the youngsters warm, contented and growing.

The final stages of weaning can be taken more leisurely with a winter litter, but the puppies should still be quite independent of their dam at six weeks. Both summer and winter litters can be safely dosed for roundworm at the age of four weeks, and again at six. Any sign of worms on the second worming will mean a third worming at eight weeks.

The purpose of this chapter is not to discourage the novice from breeding a winter litter but to draw attention to the great care and watchfulness that are called for if it is attempted. Constant vigilance and readiness to cope with a sudden spell of very cold or inclement weather, meticulous attention to the temperature of the whelping chamber, both by day and night during and after parturition, and the maintenance of whatever type of heating appliance is employed are essential. It should always be remembered that with winter-born puppies one cannot afford to take chances. A minor lapse in kennel management of a kind which in summer might pass without any ill-effects may, in winter, have serious, even fatal, results. Unless the conditions and treatment here outlined can be assured, the beginner will be well advised if possible, to delay mating a bitch which comes in season between September and December until her next heat, when the whole business of looking after the pregnant mother-to-be, whelping and rearing the puppies may be expected to offer fewer difficulties and disappointments.

INDEX